MAKE
IT
MESSY

MAKE IT MESSY

My Perfectly Imperfect Life

MARCUS SAMUELSSON

WITH VERONICA CHAMBERS

Delacorte Press

Text copyright © 2015 by Marcus Samuelsson Group, LLC.
Front jacket photograph copyright © 2015 by Paul Brissman;
back jacket photograph courtesy of the author
Photo insert courtesy of the author

All rights reserved. Published in the United States by Delacorte Press, an imprint of Random House Children's Books, a division of Random House LLC, a Penguin Random House Company, New York. This work is based on *Yes, Chef*, copyright © 2012 by Marcus Samuelsson Group LLC, published in hardcover by the Random House Publishing Group, a division of Random House LLC, in 2012.

Delacorte Press is a registered trademark and the colophon is a trademark of Random House LLC.

Visit us on the Web! randomhouseteens.com

Educators and librarians, for a variety of teaching tools, visit us at RHTeachersLibrarians.com

Library of Congress Cataloging-in-Publication Data
Samuelsson, Marcus.
Make it messy : my perfectly imperfect life /
Marcus Samuelsson with Veronica Chambers.
pages cm
ISBN 978-0-385-74400-3 (trade hardcover)
ISBN 978-0-375-99144-8 (library binding)
ISBN 978-0-385-37419-4 (ebook)
1. Cooks—United States—Biography. 2. Cooks—Sweden—Biography.
3. African American cooks—Biography. I. Chambers, Veronica. II. Title.
TX149.S28A3 2014
641.5092—dc23
2014017788

The text of this book is set in 11-point Berling.
Book design by Trish Parcell

Printed in the United States of America
10 9 8 7 6 5 4 3 2 1
First Edition

This is to the chefs and mentors I had along the way who gave me a chance. And to those who didn't give me a chance and made me prove I could do it.

And to my mother, who through all the ups and downs stood next to and behind me with strength and encouragement.

Introduction

My name is Marcus Samuelsson, and I'm a chef. This is the story of my life, from being born in Ethiopia, to being adopted by a family in Sweden, to my years playing soccer, and then eventually to becoming a chef. It's all in here—the stuff I'm proud of and the stuff I'm not so proud of, my biggest heartbreaks and the times I was so scared I threw up three times a day.

As a chef, I'm not interested in making everything perfect. I'm interested in making each dish delicious. Delicious is so much more interesting than perfect. Hence the title of this book. There were times, especially between the ages of twelve and twenty-five, when my life felt like nothing more than one mess after another. It doesn't matter that I made some messes. What matters is that I cleaned them up. I hope my journey will inspire you to go full out for your dream and to change direction and try something new if you hit a roadblock. You might see me on TV and think, "That guy eats amazing food, he hangs out with celebrities, and he's famous. His life is easy." But as you'll learn, cooking was my plan B. I had another dream entirely, and when it didn't work out, I honestly thought my life was over. But here's the thing: it ain't over till it's over. Every day is a chance to try something different.

I hope this book inspires you on your journey. If it does (and even if it doesn't), I'd love to hear from you. You can visit me online at marcussamuelsson.com, and you can holler at me on Twitter at @MarcusCooks. And if you remember nothing else from this book, please remember this: perfect is overrated. Make it messy and make it delicious.

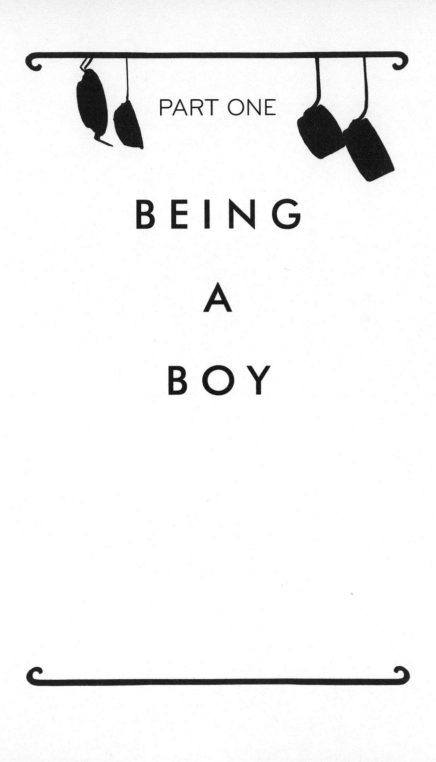

PART ONE

BEING

A

BOY

CHAPTER 1

My African Mother

I've never seen a picture of my mother.

I have traveled to her homeland, my homeland, dozens of times. I have met her brothers and sisters. I have found my birth father and eight half brothers and half sisters I didn't know I had. I have met my mother's relatives in Ethiopia, but when I ask them to describe my mother, they throw out generalities. "She was nice," they tell me. "She was pretty." "She was smart." *Nice, pretty, smart.* The words seem meaningless, except the last is a clue because even today, in rural Ethiopia, girls are not encouraged to go to school. That my mother was intelligent rings true because I know she had to be shrewd to save the lives of me and my sister, which is what she did.

Although I've never seen a picture of my mother, I know

how she cooked. For me, my mother is *berbere*, an Ethiopian spice mixture. You can use it on everything from lamb and chicken to roasted peanuts. It's Ethiopians' salt and pepper. I know she cooked with it because it's in the DNA of every Ethiopian mother. Right now, if I could, I would lead you to a red tin in my kitchen—one of dozens I keep by the stove in my apartment in Harlem—that is filled with my own blend and marked with blue electrical tape and my own illegible scrawl. I would reach into this tin and grab a handful of the red-orange powder, and hold it up to your nose so you could smell the garlic, the ginger, the sun-dried chili.

My mother didn't have a lot of money, so she fed us *shiro*. It's a chickpea flour you boil, kind of like polenta. You pour it into hot water and add butter, onions, and *berbere*. You simmer it for about forty-five minutes, until it's the consistency of hummus, and then you eat it with *injera*, a sour, rich bread made from a grain called *teff*. I know this is what she fed us because this is what poor people eat in Ethiopia. My mother carried the chickpea powder in her pocket or bag. That way, all she needed to make dinner was water and fire.

In Meki, the small farming village near where I'm from, there are no roads. We are actually from Abrugandana, a village smaller than Meki that does not exist on most maps. You go to Meki, take a right in the middle of nowhere, walk about five miles, and there's Abrugandana.

I know my mother was not taller than five feet two inches, but I also know she was not delicate. Country women in Ethiopia are strong because they walk everywhere. When I go there now, I stare at the young women and their children and it's like watching a home movie that does not exist of

6

my childhood. Each woman has a kid, which is me, on her back, and the fingers of her right hand are interlocked with another, slightly older kid's fingers, and that's my sister. Each has her food and wares in her bag, which is slung across her chest and rests on her hip. The older kid holds a bucket of water on her shoulders, a bucket that's almost as heavy as she is. That's how strong that child is.

Women like my mother don't wear shoes. They don't have shoes. My mother, my sister, and I would walk the Sidama savannah for four hours a day, to and from my mother's job selling crafts in the market. Before three p.m. it would be too hot to walk, so we would rest under a tree and gather our strength and wait for the sun to set. After eight p.m. it was dark and there were new threats—animals that would see a baby like me as supper and dangerous men who might see my mother and attack her.

I have never seen a picture of my mother, but I know her features because I have seen them staring back at me in the mirror my entire life. I know she had a cross somewhere near her face. It was a henna tattoo of a cross, henna taking the place of the jewelry she could not afford or even dream of having. There was also an Orthodox cross somewhere on the upper part of my mother's body, maybe on her neck, maybe on her chest, near her heart. She had put it there to show that she was a woman of faith. She was an Orthodox Ethiopian Christian, which is very similar to being a Catholic.

In *The Souls of Black Folk*, W. E. B. DuBois spoke of the double consciousness that African Americans are born into, the need to be able to live in both the black world and the white world. But that double consciousness is not limited to

African Americans. My mother was born into it, too. Her tribe was a minority in that section of Ethiopia, and it was essential to her survival that she spoke both the language of her village, Amhara, and the language of the greater outside community, which is Oromo. She was cautious, and when she left the Amharic village, she flipped that switch. She not only spoke Oromo, but she also spoke it with a native accent.

I was just a toddler when a tuberculosis epidemic hit Ethiopia. My mother was sick, I was sick, and my sister, Linda, was doing only slightly better than the two of us. We were all coughing up blood, and my mother had seen enough sickness in her young life to measure the ravages of the disease. She knew she had to do something. She put me on her back. It was all coming at her now: the fatigue and the fever; pieces of her lung splintering and mixing with her throw-up; the calcifications on her bones, where the disease had already spread. She and Linda walked more than seventy-five miles, my mother carrying me the whole way, under a hot sun, from our village to the hospital in Addis Ababa to get help. I don't know how many days they walked, or how sick my mother was by the time she got there. But I do know that when we arrived, there were thousands of people standing in the street, sick and dying, awaiting care. I do not know how my mother managed to get us through those lines and into that hospital. I do know that she never left that hospital and that perhaps it was only by the miracle of that henna cross that Linda and I got out alive.

⌒·⌒

Today, in the dead of night when I should be sleeping, I sometimes imagine the breath of the woman who not only gave me life but also delivered me from death. I sometimes reach into that tin by my stove and take a handful of *berbere*, sift it through my fingers, and toss it into the pan. I have taught myself the recipes of my mother's people because those foods are for me, as a chef, the easiest connection to the mysteries of who my mother was. Her identity remains stubbornly shrouded in the past, so I feed myself and the people I love the food that she made. But I cannot see her face.

CHAPTER 2

My Swedish Mother

My father wanted a son. That is how I came to live in Sweden, of all places. My sister and I were orphaned in Ethiopia in 1972, in the tuberculosis epidemic that cost my mother her life. And the Samuelssons of Göteborg, Lennart and Ann Marie, wanted a son.

They already had a daughter, an eight-year-old foster child named Anna, who had been born to a Swedish woman and a Jamaican man. While it would take decades for the United States to see a wave of international and transracial adoptions, this had been going on in Sweden since the 1950s and 1960s. In those days, it was nearly impossible to find a Swedish child to adopt. Single and pregnant Swedish women either had abortions or raised their children as single mothers, which was not frowned upon by the society at large. So in the late 1960s, my parents were matched with fifteen-month-old Anna. She was not technically adopted but was part of the family and was doted on nonetheless by Lennart and Ann Marie, who were thrilled to have their dream of becoming parents come true.

Before a family adopts a child, there's a journey they go on. For my parents, it was ten long, painful years of "We want to have a baby, but we can't." Today, if a couple is trying to get pregnant and it's not happening, doctors can do tests and, in most cases, offer up a diagnosis and sometimes a measure of hope. Back then, there was just my mother, Ann Marie, sitting in the kitchen with *her* mother, wondering how she was going to become the woman she wanted to be without a child. She wanted to have a family. She was a very traditional person in that sense. When my parents took Anna in, my mother hardly cared what race she was. Ann Marie Samuelsson, at age forty-five, was finally a mother. Anna wasn't black or white—she was joy.

In the Samuelsson family, the adoption chain goes back even further. Right after the Second World War, my mother's parents took a Jewish girl into their one-bedroom apartment. My mother was fifteen years old at the time and spoke fluent German. Sweden had remained neutral during the war, and, like many young people her age, my mother volunteered to go down to the port and work as a translator to help the thousands of Jews who were walking from Denmark to Sweden, seeking refuge. On the docks, she met a sixteen-year-old girl named Frieda. Frieda was Czechoslovakian and had been in a concentration camp. She was all alone. My mom and Frieda became friendly, and one day my mother said to my grandfather, "Can't we just take her? Can't we save one person?" My grandparents didn't have any money, but they did it: they took her in. And the happiness Frieda brought to my mother's life led to the happiness Anna brought to my parents' life, which paved the way for us.

My father wanted a son. He didn't care what color the boy was; he just wanted a boy he could teach to hike and fish. He filled out adoption forms in triplicate and considered offers from any part of the globe where orphaned baby boys were seeking homes: Greece, Vietnam, Korea, Russia, the continent of Africa. Any place that had been touched by famine or war, any place poor enough to part with an orphan.

I'd been hospitalized in Addis Ababa for six months but was on the mend when Ann Marie and Lennart got the call saying I might soon be up for adoption. It wasn't just me, though: I had my four-year-old sister, who had also been hospitalized, and our Ethiopian social worker didn't want to separate us. We had already lost our mother to disease, she told the Samuelssons; it would be best if we didn't lose each other now.

Yes, Ann Marie and Lennart said almost instantly. Yes, why not two?

It would take nearly a year for my sister and me to make the journey from Addis Ababa to Göteborg, a blue-collar city on Sweden's southwest coast.

⌒·⌒

The Friday after my father's mother died, my parents received a phone call in the Smögen house. It was my mother's

12

parents. The Swedish adoption agency, unable to reach them directly, had called with news: my sister and I were on our way from Ethiopia. My parents raced back to Göteborg, stopping along the way to purchase a bunk bed and linens, and then booked round-trip tickets to Stockholm—three going and five returning—for the next day. As our parents would always say, with both grief and gratitude, never before had they seen so clearly how when one life ends, another begins.

My mother never gave birth, but as any adoptive mother knows, the journey to meet the child you hope to call your own is its own kind of labor. When Mom, Dad, and Anna arrived at the customs area, they learned that our flight had been delayed for several hours. My father, a scientist, and Anna, the daughter who loved being by his side, sat quietly reading, while my nervous mother proceeded to unpack a picnic in the airport waiting area. A large thermos of coffee for her and Dad, a small thermos of *saft*, a sweet red-currant drink, for Anna. Then came two types of sandwiches, both on heavily margarined multigrain bread. One was made of *västerbottensost*, a hard, Parmesan-like cow's-milk cheese from northern Sweden, and a few thin slices of green pepper. The other was stuffed with slabs of a rough, country-style liver pâté. My mother's mother, Helga, had not only made the pâté but also topped it with slivers of homemade pickles and a smear of grainy mustard. For dessert, there was apple cake, which, my mother explained to anyone who would listen, would have been so much better with the traditional vanilla sauce topping, but because they had been in a rush, and had traveled by plane, compromises had to be made.

A dozen times a week, easily, I am stopped on the street

in New York City by someone, most often a woman, who tells me that she is the mother of an adopted child. More and more over the past few years, these women have adopted their children from Ethiopia and have read about me or seen me on TV and know my story. What they want to tell me is about the moment when they met their child in person for the first time. I try to be polite, but the hard thing is that after hearing so many of their stories, each a little different, it becomes difficult for me to distinguish their stories from my own. What's real and what's imagined? Was it my adoptive mother who cried when she first picked me up, or was it that woman I met a few weeks ago outside my restaurant? Was I the one who was handed an apple and spit it out because it was the very first time I'd eaten a piece of fruit, or was that my sister? Was I the one who smiled shyly and sweetly, or did I hide? The stories of the adoptive parents I've met stay with me long after we cross paths, so for accuracy, I must depend as I always have on my sister Linda. She was five and I was three, and she remembers the moment when we met our adoptive parents with far more clarity than I ever could. Here's how she describes it:

When our plane finally landed, our escort, Seney, got off first. She was tall, thin, with medium-brown skin. Very pretty Habesha, meaning someone like us, Amhara heritage. She held you on one hip and held me tightly by the hand. I didn't want to be there. A porter pushed a cart with our "luggage," a suitcase for Seney and a small cloth satchel for us. Seney handed you to Ann Marie, then opened her suitcase to present our

new parents with gifts: Ethiopian handmade crafts that
Mom still proudly displays in her living room. Seney
had no money of her own; she must have budgeted
carefully the cost of getting us to the airport and the
plane tickets, making sure to have enough so that we
could be fed in the airport if the Samuelssons were late.
But it would not have been our people's way to just
hand two foreigners these motherless kids. It would
have been important to Seney that we come bearing
more than the pale skin on our open palms.

On their flight from Göteborg to Stockholm, my parents
had chosen our Swedish names. I was born Kassahun but
would be called Marcus. My sister, Fantaye, would become
Linda. They began to call us by these names right away. My
father bent down to say hello to Linda, who vanished behind
the folds of Seney's skirt.

Linda was five, old enough to have remembered everything: our village outside Addis, our mother, the hospital
where she died, and the wards where we'd competed for
food, attention, and survival. Linda was silent all the way to
Göteborg. The only thing that gave her comfort was holding
on to a small square of tattered fabric she'd brought from
Ethiopia. She didn't cry, she remembers, because tears and
the vulnerability they symbolized were too rich a gift to give
to Lennart and Ann Marie, the man and woman she now
viewed as potential enemies because she was unsure of the
future and wanted to protect me. So she sat next to Anna in
the backseat of our parents' car while I sat in the front, sleeping in our new mother's lap.

In his application, my father promised to raise his adopted children in a good family, one with a dog and a cat, "both very friendly toward children." He described their neighborhood, Puketorp, as having about three hundred families with a surrounding forest where "we hike in the summer and ski and saucer in the winter." He promised small lakes with crystal-clear waters, perfect for skating and swimming, and a modest house with a flat lawn and an outdoor playhouse, tailor-made for "jumping and playing with balls."

The house, neighborhood, and surroundings were all as he described, but it would take more than the comparative opulence of Göteborg to win Linda over. She trusted no one except her new sister, Anna. Linda was my protector. If our new mom reached down to pick me up without securing Linda's permission first, Linda would pry me out of her arms and scold my mother in Amharic. Each time my mother tried to put me into the bathtub, a frightful contraption with a mad gush of water, the likes of which we'd never seen before, Linda would cling to me so tightly that my father would have to lift the two of us, stuck together like conjoined twins, and drop us into the tub together until we finally adjusted.

My mother learned to ask Linda's permission each and every time she wanted to make contact with me. Mom spoke to Linda in Swedish, enunciating each word carefully and raising the volume a notch or two, as if that might help. With a mime's gift for hand gestures and facial expressions, my new mother each day made herself more easily understood, and after many months, Linda loosened her grip.

There is an Ethiopian fairy tale called "The Lion's Whiskers." It's the story of a woman who was in an unhappy marriage. Her husband came home from work late every day, and some nights he did not come home at all. Distraught, the wife went to see the village elder. He assured her that he could fix this trouble. "I will prepare a medicine that will make your husband love you with an unbounded devotion," he said.

The woman could barely contain her excitement. *"Abba,"* she begged, using the word for a man who is father to the entire village, "make the potion right away."

The elder shook his head. "I need one essential ingredient and it is not an easy one to get," he explained. "You must provide me with a whisker plucked from a living lion."

The woman was in love and unafraid. She said, "I will get it for you."

It was not the elder's wish to cause the woman any harm. On the contrary, he had lived a long time and he believed that in asking her for an ingredient that was as fantastical as fairy dust, he was letting her down easy. Some things were the way they were and always had been. Husbands got bored and sometimes came home late or not at all. Time had taught the elder that his most important job was not to mix potions but to listen. For a woman who is anxious and lonely, the reassuring counsel of an elder was its own kind of balm.

But that was not the case with this woman, for when she loved, she loved fiercely.

The next day, she took a slab of raw meat down to the river, where she had, on many occasions, watched a lion take his morning drink. She was afraid, but she found the courage to walk up close and throw the meat to the lion. Each morning, she returned and fed the beast, getting closer and closer to him until, one day, she was able to sit by his side and, with no danger to herself at all, pluck the whisker from the lion's cheek. When she returned to the village elder, he was shocked that she had completed the seemingly impossible task.

"How did you do it?" he asked.

The woman explained, and at the end of her story, the village elder spoke to her with deference and respect. "You have the courage, patience, and grace to befriend a lion," he said. "You need no potion to fix your marriage."

This is a fairy tale that all children in Ethiopia learn, but for me, it is also the story of my early days in Sweden and how my sister and I became Samuelssons. The brave woman was my mother, Ann Marie, and Linda was the lion.

CHAPTER 3

Swedish Fish

My love for food did not come from my mother.

For my mom, putting dinner on the table was just another thing to get done in the course of a long, busy day.
Cooking competed with ferrying her three kids back and
forth to soccer, ice-skating lessons, horseback riding, doctors'
and dentists' appointments. Once I became old enough to
test my daredevil skills (Dad wanted a boy!) on my skateboard and bike, there were regular visits to the emergency
room as well.

It's not that my mother was a *bad* cook; she simply didn't
have the time. In the late 1970s, she subscribed to a magazine
that had "try it at home" recipes for the busy homemaker,
slightly exotic concoctions that featured canned, frozen, and

boxed ingredients. This was her go-to source of inspiration. She made pasta as not even a prisoner would tolerate it, with tinny tomato sauce and mushy frozen peas. She served roast pork from imaginary Polynesian shores, with canned pineapple rings and homemade curry whipped cream. She wanted us to eat well, to experience other cultures, but she also didn't want to be tied to the stove the way her mother had been. Her mother, Helga, had worked as a maid since the age of eleven, and now, even in retirement, was unable to break the habit of cooking and serving, cooking and serving. My mother saw that and ran the other way.

What she valued in a meal was convenience. It's funny that the one dish of hers I adored was the one that could not be rushed: cabbage rolls. I loved sitting on the counter and watching as she blanched the cabbage leaves, seasoned the ground pork with salt and pepper, then scooped the pork into the leaves, wrapping them like cigars and placing them carefully on a platter. My mother's cabbage rolls were special because the very preparation of the dish forced her to slow down so I could enjoy her presence as much as her cooking. The literal translation for *dim sum*, small Chinese dumplings and snacks, is "little bits of heart." My mother's cabbage rolls were my dim sum.

My mother organized our dinners the way she organized the household—efficiency and routine ruled the day. No more than ten dishes made it into her regular rotation. On Mondays, we had meatballs with mashed potatoes, lingonberries, and gravy. On Tuesdays, herring. On Wednesdays, a roast. On Thursdays, we ate split pea soup, and on Fridays, fish casserole. Once in a while, we veered from the routine. But not often.

Tuesdays I loved most of all. That was the day the fishmonger drove his beat-up Volvo panel truck into our neighborhood's modest shopping area, which consisted of a tailor we never used, a grocery store owned by the Blomkvists, and the newsstand guy from whom I could occasionally cadge a peppermint and where my father bought canisters of loose tobacco and cigarette papers.

My mother always took me with her to the fishmonger on Tuesdays, but not before raking a comb through my hair, yanking so hard that for the next hour, I could feel the aftershocks on my scalp. My laces had to be tied, my freshly ironed shirt tucked in. My mother dressed up, too: lipstick, a leather purse, and a sharp red felt cap that she thought gave her a more sophisticated air.

We would both watch as the fish man, Mr. Ljungqvist, parked his truck at the curb in front of the Blomkvists' market and unfurled his blue-and-white-striped awning. Mr. Ljungqvist was shaped like a bowling ball, with thick white hair curling out from under his black fisherman's cap. He wore a sweater under his smock and a red apron on top. No matter how cold it was, his pink hands were bare, chafed and scraped from handling so much ice, sharp belly scales, and spiny fins.

I liked to hoist myself on the bottom lip of the service window and see what was waiting on Mr. Ljungqvist's icy deathbed. It never turned out to be anything too exciting—some cod, some perch, some *sill*, which is what we called herring—but I always hoped he'd procured something more surprising and exotic from the bottom of the sea, like an eel or turbot or squid. But there were no surprises as to what

21

my mother would buy or how my mother might cook it. The big, oafy-looking cod would be ground into fish balls. Perch would be broiled and served with butter and lemon. And the herring? The herring was our hamburger.

Herring is the classic Swedish fish. It was on almost every table at every meal, figured into almost every course but dessert, and showed up at every holiday. It was even woven into the language. You could be deaf as a herring or dumb as a herring. Tram conductors who carried trolleys full of commuters were called herring packers. If you were exhausted, you were a dead herring. Smelly shoes were called herring barrels.

Ljungqvist's customers bought lots and lots of herring—to poach, pickle, bake, and layer into cheesy, creamy casseroles with leeks and tomatoes. On the nights my mother would fry the herring, she bypassed the ten-inch-long Atlantic herring in favor of the smaller, silver-skinned *strömming* that came from the Baltic Sea and fit better in her cast-iron pan. As a Swedish woman who came of age in the 1950s, she could have happily served mushy peas from the tin, but she scaled, gutted, and filleted the herring herself. For her, that wasn't a kitchen skill. Knowing how to clean a fish was as innate as knowing how to open a door.

I helped my mother pick out our fish. What you wanted to avoid at all costs were cloudy eyes and blood spots on their gills, telltale signs that the fish was not fresh. My father, who had grown up in a family of fishermen, did not trust my mother to pick the fish. It was *my* job, he told me secretly, to make sure she made the right choices. When we found the acceptable choice for that night's supper, Mom nodded to me, I nodded to Mr. Ljungqvist, and he picked the fish out of the ice, added it to the others he had laid into the crook of one arm, and wrapped them in newspaper.

Next, my mom would pick out the anchovies for our Friday night dinner, Jansson's Temptation, a casserole of potato, anchovy, onion, and cream. Mr. Ljungqvist dug into a shallow pail of anchovies with his red scoop, then shook out the extras until he had exactly the right amount. They glimmered, metallic and shiny, against the ice. Put that one back, my mother would say. No, no, I want *that* one.

Learning how to pick the freshest fish for the best value helped lay the groundwork for my work as a chef. And as my sisters did not accompany us on these fish-buying expeditions, they would never know that, occasionally, despite her virulent anti-sweets policy, our mother could be swayed. Every once in a while, after we'd made our purchases from Mr. Ljungqvist, I would talk her into walking over to the newsstand and buying a little candy. Salted licorice for her. Colored sour balls for me.

CHAPTER 4

Grandma Helga

After my parents adopted Anna, my mother's parents, wanting to be nearby and to help in any way they could, moved to Göteborg from the southern province of Skåne. They bought a small one-bedroom house just a few minutes away by bike, close enough that we crossed paths several times a day. We called Helga and Edvin Jonsson *Mormor* and *Morfar*—terms of respect that translate to "mother's mother" and "mother's father"—and loved them like the adoring set of bonus parents that they were.

At Mormor's, the smell of food was omnipresent: the yeasty aroma of freshly baked bread or the tang of drying rose hips hit you as soon as you walked in. Something was always going on in her kitchen, and usually several things at once. My grandmother would start chopping vegetables for dinner while sterilizing jars for canning, while stirring a pot of chicken stock or grinding pork for a month's worth of sausages. If I had to try to pinpoint my earliest food memory, it would not be a single taste but a smell—my grandmother's house.

Before moving to Göteborg, my grandmother lived where she had grown up, in the province of Skåne. To say a person comes from Skåne carries a lot of meaning for a Swede. At the southernmost tip of the country, Skåne is to Sweden, in many ways, what Provence is to France. With the mildest climate and the most fertile soil in Sweden, it is the country's chief agricultural region. Not surprisingly, Skåne has always been known for its rich culinary landscape, a landscape that gave birth to a generation of instinctively inventive cooks. My grandmother was no exception. She spent so much of her time at the stove that when I close my eyes and try to remember her, it's an image of her back that I see first. She would toss smiles and warm welcomes over her shoulder, never fully taking her eyes off the pots she was tending.

Mormor had the unique experience of being surrounded by luxury despite living in poverty her entire life. Her work as a maid for upper-class Swedish families had kept food on the table for her family through the lean years surrounding the rationing of two World Wars. From the families she worked for, she learned how to make restaurant-worthy meals. This kind of training, coupled with her own thriftiness, meant that she made almost everything we ate from scratch and wasted almost nothing; her pantry was so well stocked that I barely remember her shopping. Maybe she'd send me out to get sugar or she'd go to the fishmonger herself, but otherwise, everything she needed seemed to appear, as if by magic, from her pantry or emerge from the garden that she tended with the same careful devotion that she used to prepare our family's big Saturday suppers.

Mormor's one indulgence was wallpaper. The walls of her house were covered in exuberant flowers, exploding colors, and bold vertical stripes. But other than that, her house was simple and quiet, much quieter than ours. You could open the door and know that no children lived there: there was just the low murmur of my grandfather listening to the news on the radio and my grandmother clanking away in the kitchen. She did all her prep work by hand and preferred mortar and pestle to the electric mixers and blenders my mother bought her in the hopes of making her life easier. She was suspicious of newfangled inventions. Having cooked most of her adult life on a wood-burning stove, she never entirely warmed to the electric oven in her modern kitchen.

Mormor treated her house like it was her own little food factory. She made everything herself: jams, pickles, and breads. She bought large cuts of meat or whole chickens and game animals from the butcher, and then she broke them down into chops and roasts at home. It's so funny to me how, today, we celebrate braising as some refined, elegant approach, when it's the same slow-cooking method Mormor used. Her menus followed a simple logic:

You have bread today because it's fresh.

You have toast tomorrow because the bread has gone stale.

You make croutons the next day, and whatever bread is

left after that gets ground into crumbs that you'll use to batter fish.

In the United States, the best-known Swedish dish is meatballs, but pickles and jams connect the dots of Swedish cuisine and make an appearance in almost every meal and dish. At breakfast, we'd pour buttermilk over granola and sweeten it with black-currant jam. A favorite summer dessert was ice cream topped with gooseberry preserves, and a late-night TV snack would be toast with cheese and jams. Seared herring would be served with lingonberry jam, and liver pâté sandwiches were topped with pickled cucumbers.

Swedes traditionally prefer a pickle that is salty, sour, and quite sweet. To achieve that blend of flavors, we use a solution called 1-2-3: one part vinegar, two parts sugar, three parts water. But for the pickle to be truly Swedish, the vinegar has to be *ättika*, a beech-wood-based product that has a sinus-clearing, eye-tearing bite to it, twice as acidic as American vinegars. Mormor spent an enormous amount of time pickling and preserving, using the 1-2-3 solution to pickle cauliflowers and cucumbers, herrings and beets, which she stuffed into jars and stored in her pantry.

Pantry is almost too fancy a word for where Mormor stored her food. Hers was a closet at the foot of the basement stairs. A pull-chain light hung from the ceiling, and the single bulb revealed a space so small that by the time I was ten years old, it was no longer a viable option for me in our games of hide-and-seek. The closet doubled as a root cellar, with burlap sacks of potatoes lining the floor along one wall. Above them were shelves of savory foods—pickled onions, cucumbers, beets, and different types of herring: *strömming, sill,* and the store-bought *matjes* herring, prized for its delicate, less fishy flavor. The far wall held the sweet preserves, which were placed in rows that went back three jars deep. Each was covered with a handwritten label that stated the contents and the date that it was canned.

Mormor made jams from the berries she grew in her front yard as well as from what she found in the woods near our house, like lingonberries, the quintessential Swedish fruit, which have a texture and tang similar to cranberries. She preserved cloudberries, black currants, raspberries, and gooseberries; and made jam from apples, pears, and plums, all of which came from her own trees. That dark little closet was my grandmother's version of a jewelry case, and the bright jellies and jams were her gemstones.

⌒·⌒

I loved Saturdays as a kid. We were lucky. Saturdays meant soccer practice for me, ice-skating and riding lessons for my sisters, and almost without exception, Saturdays meant the best meal we would have all week because dinner was almost always at my grandparents' house. As soon as I got home from soccer, I would jump on my bike and speed over to Mormor's house. It took me exactly seven minutes to cut across the nature preserve that abutted our property, speed down the road on the other side, and make it up the long driveway to my grandparents' house. I dumped the bike at the foot of their steps, took the stairs two at a time, and walked as fast as I could to Mormor's kitchen. There was *no* running in my grandmother's house. She'd look at me standing there out of breath and say, "Ah, there you are. Come.

I have a job for you." She would pull out a stool and set me to stringing rhubarb or shelling peas or plucking a chicken. My sisters never joined us in our Saturday-afternoon cooking sessions, and I was only too happy to have Mormor to myself.

Her signature dish was roast chicken, which meant chicken soup the next day. It was yummy, the perfect food, warm like the kind of hug only a grandmother can give. Looking back, I realize that my grandmother's food was my introduction to rustic cooking. It had more levels of flavor than a twelve-year-old could understand. She had no culinary training and didn't know how to build textures the way chefs build texture, but she got it. In her *body*, she knew how to create those levels.

Growing up in Skåne, my grandmother had learned to kill a chicken old-school style. Grab the bird, knife to the neck. Like, "Come here, boom." You learn to respect food in a different way when you have to kill it yourself, she would say. I never forgot that lesson, even though when I was a kid we didn't kill the chickens we ate for dinner. But the fresh birds my grandmother purchased still looked like birds— they had feet and feathers, and we had to handle them and pluck them ourselves. It was something I became good at, too, the kind of tedious work that needs to be done carefully and quickly, and that would one day prepare me for the lower levels of professional kitchens.

After we plucked the chicken, my grandmother would salt it generously. Right there, she created a level of flavor. So why did she salt it? Because even though she had a refrigerator, she wasn't *raised* with a refrigerator. In her mind, she couldn't be sure how many days the chicken would last.

And what happens when you salt something? The skin gets firmer. You've preserved it and the meat gets more tender. Right there, she was creating texture.

After she salted it, she would put the chicken in the basement and leave it there for a couple of hours, because that's where it was cold and dry. As a chef, you would leave the chicken by the air conditioner so the skin gets dry, which will help you when you roast it. Same basic principle. She had these intuitive chef moves that are taught in culinary school.

When she was ready to cook the chicken, she would show me how to add spices—cardamom, ginger, coriander seeds—that we'd grind and rub all over the skin. Then she would put carrots in the roasting dish, making a little bed for the chicken to sit on. She would stuff the bird with ingredients that came from her own yard: rosemary, apples, onions, maybe a little garlic. She'd sew the chicken up and put it in the oven. While it was roasting, she'd get going on the stock. Everything that was left over—the extra skin, the neck, the giblets—would go into the pot for stock. Then she'd put any vegetable scraps into the pot, too, and let it all simmer.

Mormor had this bad Chinese soy sauce, which was the best she could get in Sweden in the 1970s. She'd say, "I don't like white sauce. Gravy has to have color." Mormor thought like a chef. She wanted the food to be not only tasty but also beautiful to look at. She'd take a pan, the drippings, flour, and soy sauce, and make gravy. She wasn't raised with butter, because she couldn't afford it, so she cooked with grease fat. That was the flavor she put into a lot of her gravies and sauces. Then she'd take a few tablespoons of the stock she'd just made and use that to thin out the gravy. She'd hand me a slotted spoon and say, "Okay, Marcus, get the lumps out."

Later that night, she'd serve the meal we'd created, always giving credit to "my little helper." No matter how many times we prepared the same dish the same way, I was always excited to see the meal I'd helped to make, presented formally on a silver serving tray: chicken roasted with rosemary, accompanied by carrots glazed with a little bit of honey, ginger, and sugar.

My mother, my father, my sisters, and I would often come back the next day for chicken soup. Mormor would take all the meat that was left over from the Saturday night supper and add it to the stock along with a boiled pot of rice or potatoes. And that was the meal. It was so full of flavor because of her upbringing, the poverty that she came from. The preserving technique that made everything taste richer, deeper. The fresh chicken that she had hand-picked from the market. Drying the bird, which gives you the perfect skin. The salting because she never trusted refrigerators, the two or three days' worth of meals that she would create from one chicken because being poor makes you inventive.

The roasted chicken I make today is an homage to hers. I have luxuries that she didn't. I use corn-fed chicken. I use real butter instead of grease fat. But the layering of flavor and the techniques? They're all hers.

CHAPTER 5

With Respect to the Sea

Every spring, my father would take a trip to Smögen, the island off the west coast of Sweden where he was born and raised and where our family spent most of our vacations. Every Easter break, he drove there alone to prepare the summerhouse and the family's fishing boats. I was twelve, just about to start middle school, when he invited me along for the first time.

"This is not a holiday," he warned. "We are going to get the boats ready. You can't come along unless you're willing to help."

During the summer, Smögen was flooded with tourists who came to see Sweden's longest boardwalk and eat prawn sandwiches from brightly colored wooden huts, which, from afar, looked like they were made of Popsicle sticks. But this was not summer and we were not tourists. In March in Smögen, the salt air coated your skin, and its gritty texture made you feel tougher, both inside and out. "Just us two men," my father said, my father, who had so longed for a son that he had flown paper planes—adoption forms in triplicate—all the way to Africa to make his dream come true.

The road from Göteborg to Smögen was a patchy two-lane that changed from rugged shoreline to thick forests of pines and spruce to meadows full of yarrow and twinflower. Sometimes there was no vegetation at all, and the road cut through vast rock formations, endless fields of dark gray granite that looked, from the car window, like elephant hide. I knew we were close when I saw the first cluster of red-roofed houses, the docks, the bobbing boats, the small beach, and the steely water of the fjord that would eventually spill into the sea. And then I saw it, the first sign that we had arrived: a white two-story house with a red roof, set back from the road, with no other houses around.

This was the house of my great-uncle Torsten, my father's uncle and the closest thing I had to a paternal grandfather since my father's father had died before I was even born. Torsten's house sat at the foot of the new bridge, one that hadn't existed when my father was a boy. To get to school each day, he'd had to row himself and his three siblings forty minutes each way across this inlet of the Baltic. I wondered what sort of prayers he must have said on stormy days when his boat seemed so small and the fjord seemed so wide.

Our family's house was a three-story wood-frame Victorian built in the 1800s. The house could sleep forty; back when my grandmother was alive, she ran it as a boarding-house for fishermen, feeding them and doing their laundry.

My father's entire academic career had been designed to escape this hard fisherman's life, but I could tell from the way he inspected the rooms, cranked up the radiators, cast his gaze toward the sea, and breathed deep in the cold salt air that my father had missed Smögen. That, in fact, he'd been counting the days until he could get back.

⚓

I woke up at five-thirty the next morning to the sound of a radio news program and the smell of hot chocolate. Groggy, I walked into the dark kitchen just as my father's best friend, Stellan, burst through the back door. In Hasselösund, which was the tiny community where my father was from in Smögen, no one bothered to knock or call before coming over.

Stellan had been a *yrkesfiskare*, a professional fisherman, for twenty-five years. The punishing sixteen-hour days out in the boats were like too many rounds in a boxing ring. They made his body sore in ways that sleep and ointments could never fix. He now held the less demanding role of handyman for the Smögen elementary school. As soon as my dad started speaking to Stellan, he lost his city accent. He no longer sounded so intellectual, choosing instead to speak in a local dialect so thick I could barely follow along. I sat at the table and ate the breakfast my mother had packed—orange marmalade and sliced *hushållsost*, a mild farmer's cheese, on a triangle of rye crispbread—and I listened, picking up a word here and there. My dad and Stellan drank coffee and talked about how well the fish were biting, what mackerel was going for at the local fish auction, and what we were about to do with the boats. They talked about the sea, always with great deference to its power. My father's father died at age fifty, on a boat, and it had scared my father, I think. It made him want to go to university, to make a living with his head, not his hands. He wasn't afraid of hard work and he wanted to work outside, but he didn't want a fisherman's life. Geology was a way out.

It was a three-minute walk to our boathouse. Like every other boathouse in Hasselösund, ours was painted a carnelian red with an even darker red pitched roof and white trim around the eaves, doors, and windows. The houses were small, not much bigger than the average American two-car garage, and arrayed in a perfect line up and down the pebbly beach. Inside was our boat and a mishmash of tackle: nets, traps, rods and buckets, buoys and oars and fish knives. When I got a little older, my father promised, we would also store water skis there.

The day before our arrival, Stellan had drowned the boats, pulling each one out about four feet from shore and filling it with rocks until the hull filled with water. The boats had been out of the water all winter, so the aim was to make the wood swell, which in turn would make it easier to shave off the old paint in preparation for a fresh coat.

My great-uncles Ludvig and Torsten met us at the boathouse, and they, Stellan, and Dad waded into the water, wearing rubber boots that came up to their thighs. They surrounded each boat and, on the count of three, pushed and pulled it up to the shore as cold, brackish water sloshed out. They tilted it to one side, dumping out the rocks and the last of the water, then inverted it over two thick boards they'd laid out on the beach.

I grabbed my own scraper and joined the men as we took the paint off each boat until it revealed its shell of plain wood. Every once in a while, Ludvig might correct my grip or Stellan would remind me to go along the grain of the wood instead of across it. We kept going until each boat was as brown and smooth as a walnut shell. In the hours that I worked, my father said nothing, but I basked in his smile—so much more relaxed and easy than it ever was at home.

Uncle Torsten was a tall man, easily clearing six feet, and he kept his wiry salt-and-pepper hair tamed and slicked back with plentiful amounts of grease and the comb he holstered in his pocket. For nearly fifty years he had supported his family by wrestling his living from the sea, and it showed in the deep lines and dark tan of his face. He had hard, rough hands, a ready laugh, and an easy grin, and he smelled, alternately, of tobacco and alcohol, musky and sweet. He was, to my mind, a Swedish version of the Marlboro Man.

Torsten was a strong old man. Freaky strong. Farmer strong. Even after he'd retired from fishing, he could lift an *eka*, a stout wooden rowboat, and flip it onto its blocks, by himself, as easily as a mother turns a baby over to change his or her diaper. By this time—he must have been in his late sixties—Torsten earned his living as a handyman for summering Norwegian tourists and the island's fish processing plant, Hållöfisk. He wore paint-splattered overalls and balanced a ladder on his bicycle as he rode from job to job. He also loved a stiff drink. He had this thermos of black coffee spiked with homemade vodka, and he carried it with him everywhere. When friends visited him from the city, they brought him Jack Daniel's, a rare and luxurious treat. But Torsten, deep down, was a man of simple tastes and comforts: he liked his vodka moonshine better than anything you could buy in a store.

Later, I'd think of men like Torsten and Stellan often as I made my way up the punishing ladder of the world's finest kitchens. Those Smögen men, and I count my father among them, were unafraid of hard work. They were their own doctors, therapists, and career counselors. I constantly reminded myself that they would never quit a job because of the name-calling and plate-throwing and brutal hours that are common in a professional kitchen. I made it my business to be tough in the ways that they were tough—on the inside, where it counted.

⊂·⊃

The best memories of that first trip alone with my father to Smögen were when Torsten invited me to his smokehouse. My time spent in the kitchen with Mormor, combined with my own growing passion for food, had me intrigued by the process of culinary transformation: How did you take one thing and end up with something so different? Uncle Torsten's smokehouse—the mysterious, rectangular wooden building at the back of his yard—was as important as any course I would take in culinary school. Here, I could watch that transformation occur.

There was a loop of rope where the door handle should have been, and when I pulled it open, a surge of smoke practically sucked all the air out of my lungs. The fire pit was a smoldering oil drum in the center of the room. Torsten tugged on a pipe while he smoked the fish: tobacco smoke mixing with the pungent smell of the curing solution (a liquid mixture that contains nitrate or nitrate chemicals that help cook and preserve the fish) mixing with the driftwood smoke to create the kind of odor that penetrates deep into your skin and clings to your clothes through several washings. I remember, as I stood there, thanking God my father and I had come on this trip to Smögen alone. My mother, as friendly as she was with Torsten, would have had a fit. More than once during our visits to Smögen, we'd seen or heard of a family's smokehouse blowing up like a meth lab. The men were careful, but the buildings were old and makeshift. Without official regulations or inspections, they were also unsafe.

The floor was littered with spare rods, old fish skin, and the odd pieces of stone that Torsten occasionally dropped into the drum with a clank and a hiss. Six or seven metal rods hooked into the side walls and spanned the width of the room; each rod could hold up to forty fish. Depending on the day's catch, Torsten cured eel, herring, or mackerel. Eel was a rarity and therefore highly prized, but my favorite was the mackerel, which the smoking process magically transformed from a stripy gray and green to a shimmering gold and black.

Hanging with Torsten in his smokehouse was more than a way to spend the afternoon. It was an initiation of sorts, into manhood. Chest puffed up, I stoked the fire, yanked fish off rods, and piled up stones. Torsten talked the whole time, loud and clear, always telling me what he was doing, asking me if I understood the process, what came next, why we did what we did.

"Low heat, close the door, leave it overnight."

"I've done this before, Uncle Torsten."

"Come back every other hour," he ordered. "Check the wood." He handed me a pan of cured fish. "Has your father caught any mackerel lately?"

"We brought in twenty-five this morning," I told him.

Torsten raised an eyebrow. "Well," he said, smiling. "Your father's been down in Göteborg a long time. No one can hold such a modest number against him."

My great-aunt Nini, Torsten's wife, shouted from the back door of the house, "Are we ever going to get any fish? Time for lunch, already!"

"Finally, she appears," Torsten said as he handed me two more smoked mackerel.

In the kitchen, Nini had laid out four open-faced sandwiches: sliced boiled eggs, roe paste (fish eggs that have been mixed with a red chili paste to add a sharp flavor to the meal), mayonnaise, and a sprinkling of chives on a piece of brown bread. With a knife, she quickly filleted the mackerel, dressed it with black pepper and garlic, and topped each piece of bread with the warm, flavorful fish.

I carried Torsten's plate over to the table, placing it in front of him. He took a bite, and I could see in his face the pleasure he took in the rich simplicity of the meal: the flaky chunks of fish, the velvety texture of the egg, the saltiness of the roe. Then he closed his eyes. "That's a good life," he said.

Torsten and Nini had a louder, more brash style than my parents, and I loved to watch the way they mirrored each other. Their shouts and seemingly exasperated murmurs were the words of two old people who had stood, united, against the harshness of the cold blue sea for so many years and made a life together. I looked at the two of them and the simple but hugely satisfying meals they shared, and I thought, Torsten is right. That *is* a good life.

⌒⌒

At five o'clock on our last night in Smögen, my father and I walked down the hill to visit Ludvig. He had been widowed young and lived by himself on the top floor of a large house that had tenants on the first floor and nothing going on, as far as I could tell, on the floor in between. Stellan had dropped off some mackerel earlier in the day and Ludvig was halfway through cleaning it when we walked in. He'd gutted the fish and cut off their heads; then my father took over, sharpening a thin, curved knife on a block of stone and deftly slicing the flesh off the bone.

"Marcus, if you don't cook, we don't eat," my father joked.

It was a joke, of course, because my father knew I needed no prompting to cook, which is probably why he let me take over the meal. This was my first time cooking on my own, as opposed to helping my grandmother or mother. Just as I had with the boats, I was eager to show I was a big man, that I didn't need anyone's help. I quickly washed some potatoes, then boiled them in a pot of salted water with dill, just like Mormor did. My father had brought our frying pan from home and I set it on the stove, put the flame on high, then added a large knob of butter, which slowly melted at the center. While I waited for the pan to heat up, and for the butter to bubble and turn golden, I dipped each fillet in a mix of flour, bread crumbs, salt, and pepper. I waited until the butter was good and hot, and I tested it the way I'd seen Helga do many times, by scraping into the pan a tiny bit of flour that had caked on my finger. When the flour sizzled and popped, I laid in the strips of fish, side by side. I knew then, maybe for the first time, that I wasn't just my grandmother's little helper. I had absorbed some of her gift for the movements and the timing, but the sense of how to make the meal taste *just* right—more salt, less pepper—came naturally to me, even without Mormor there to supervise me.

My father and Uncle Ludvig drank beers and spoke in their dialect while I cooked, and they didn't seem to notice that I had put the dill in with the fish too soon, so it was a crispy black by the time I retrieved it from the pan. The meal was more than the thrown-together ingredients that we'd eaten the entire week; it was a reward for a week of hard work: quick, delicious food for hungry, hardworking people.

We ate the potatoes and the fish, and I was proud to have not only helped my father do his work, but also to have prepared the workingman's simple meal. The next day, as I helped my father give the boats a light sanding and a final coat of paint, I thought of what Uncle Torsten had said about our mackerel lunch and how much he might have enjoyed the supper I had prepared. Although I was still a kid and years away from any thought of becoming a chef, I was learning the beauty of food within a context: how important it is to let the dishes be reflective of your surroundings. Hot smoked-mackerel sandwiches on dark brown bread in the smokehouse with Torsten. Panfried fish and potatoes with my father at the end of a long, hard day. If the ingredients are fresh and prepared with love, they are bound to be satisfying.

"Marcus," my father called out after me when the last boat was done. *"Val gjort, lille yrkesfiskare."* Well done, little fisherman.

CHAPTER 6

Mats

It wasn't until I'd started grade school that the question of race became real for me and my sister Linda, in large part because Anna had integrated the Samuelsson household years before we arrived. For Anna, biracial and fair-skinned with an Afro that could have rivaled Angela Davis's, the arrival of two dark-skinned siblings was a revelation. At nine years of age, she had never known children who were browner than she was. In those first few days, she would stroke my cheek and run her hands through my woolly hair, curiosity overriding her Swedish reserve. We might have been a novelty to my oldest sister, but because of Anna, Linda and I were never the "black kids" in the family. We were two *more* black kids in the family. All the skin touching and hair pulling and curious questions came to Anna first, and by the time we arrived, it went without saying that this was a mixed-race family. As a black girl in Sweden, Anna always stood out. But she handled it all in her own elegant way, in part because my mother and her birth parents, who lived nearby, never made race an issue. We were Samuelssons now, and that was all they felt they, or anybody else, needed to know.

Once we got to school, there were comments, at first more curious than cruel. And as I got older, as a boy, there was more than my fair share of taunts and playground fights. Still, it's important that you know that growing up black in Sweden was different from growing up black in America. I have had the good fortune not to have big race wounds. And I owe that to Ann Marie Samuelsson.

We had arrived in the early 1970s, in what was then a small, working-class Scandinavian city, but my mother wanted to do more than make us Samuelssons; she wanted to embrace black culture however she could. Because Anna's birth father was Jamaican, my mother spent what little pocket money she had on Bob Marley records. I can still picture her singing along to Bob as she stirred her spaghetti and peas. When Linda and I showed up, Ann Marie added Miriam Makeba to the mix. Makeba was not exactly Ethiopian—not Ethiopian at all—but was African and beautiful all the same. Even now, I can't hear a song like "Three Little Birds" without thinking of my mother blasting her music, like she blasted her love, out loud.

I might have looked on my childhood differently if I hadn't met Mats Carestam. He's my oldest friend. We met when I was five years old, and I realized there was only one kid in the neighborhood who was as good at soccer as I was. That was Mats, and I knew, even then, that we were going to either hate each other or become the best of friends.

We became best friends.

From the beginning, my battles were his battles. Which was great because Mats was the guy you wanted on your side in any kind of brawl. It's not so much that he had a quick temper. It's more that he was always this big kid who was never afraid to get down in it. No matter how nicely his mother had dressed him before he left the house, within minutes the knees of his pants would be muddy and grass-stained, and he'd be a mess. His shins were always a collage of bruises. Whenever I think of Mats, even today, I picture him wiping the back of his hand across his face and all over his clothes like a kid in a laundry-detergent commercial.

I ate at Mats's house as often as I ate at my own, and I lived for his mother's creamy macaroni and cheese. A dish like that was way too modern for my mother. Mats's mother served store-bought meatballs, which my mother would *never* do. My mother didn't love to cook, but certain things she would never cut corners on. There was also a generational gap between our families. Mats's parents were much younger, more on the go, much more contemporary.

Everything Mats ate, he covered in ketchup. Which was fine with his parents, but always left me slightly bewildered. How could you taste the cheese or the meat or the potatoes when it was drowning in cold red tomato sauce? And Mats would eat fast. He'd make himself a giant plate of mac and cheese, meatballs, pickles, and lingonberries, cover the whole thing with ketchup, and wash it down with a pint of milk in about two minutes. Mats didn't care what you put in front of him as long as there was plenty of it. He was a big kid and he ate not out of greed but because his body was this *machine* that demanded it.

It helped that my best friend was built like a tank when we started junior high school. I'd long healed from the tuberculosis, and the distended belly of poverty was gone, but I was still built like an Ethiopian runner—lean and wiry. In my mind, I was as cool and powerful as any of the American black men we saw on TV, but in the land of Vikings, I stood out as a scrawny little kid.

<hr />

One day after school, Mats and I were headed to his house for an afternoon of listening to music, reading soccer magazines, and chowing down on the kind of packaged pastries and soda my mother never had in our house. We'd made it halfway across the school playground when a basketball hit me in the back so hard that I stumbled forward.

"Hey, Marcus, why don't you teach us how to play *negerboll*," a kid named Boje called out.

It was always a little hard to tell if Boje was honestly mean-spirited or if he'd been drafted to play the part because he was a big, muscular kid, even in the sixth grade, like a nightclub bouncer. In either case, he was the closest we had to a bully at our school and I'd been lucky enough to escape his attention. Until now.

Negerboll. The word hung in the air as the boys around us, all kids in our class, froze. There couldn't have been more than twenty boys in the group, but I felt like there were a hundred eyes on me. Boje had thrown the ball hard, but the word had hit me harder. Mats picked the ball up and stood protectively in front of me, but the word kept bouncing up and down against the pavement:

Neger

Boll.

Neger

Boll.

Neger

Boll.

Although it sounded like *nigger* and Boje spewed it with that level of venom, *neger* was the Swedish word for *Negro.* There was even a Swedish cookie called *negerboll,* or, in English, *Negro ball:* it was made from cocoa powder, sugar, and oats. But Boje was not calling me a cookie. And he had thrown a basketball at me, which I took as its own kind of loaded symbol. It was the early 1980s, the dawn of the Michael Jordan era, and most Swedes associated that orange ball with dark-skinned men.

Boje wasn't done with me yet. "What, does the *neger* not know how to play *negerboll?*"

Mats picked up Boje's basketball and looked like he might shove it down the tall blond boy's throat.

"Leave him alone," Mats growled.

Later, back at Mats's house, all my clever, cutting retorts would come at me in a kind of beautiful wave, like the way genius mathematicians scrawl numbers and letters on chalkboards in movies. But in the moment, the very first time in my life someone called me out as *neger,* I had said nothing. I had spent years growing in the quiet confidence of being

47

Ann Marie and Lennart's son. I knew that they did not look like me and that I had come from a faraway place called Africa, but it was no more mysterious for me than it was for kids who still believed they had arrived on their parents' doorstep by stork. When Boje called me a *neger*, when he threw an American basketball at me and tried to hurt me, physically and emotionally, I asked myself for the very first time: *Was* I different? How was I different? And in the same way that five-year-old Linda had kept vigilant for months on end, the question occurred to me for the first time: Where was home? Was this place it?

That night, when I described the incident to my family at the dinner table, my father seemed concerned, but my mother jumped right in with what she thought was a viable solution: *"Kalla honom vit kaka,"* she said. "Call him a white cookie."

I moaned and tried to explain that it would not have the same effect. But my mother, like the mother of bullied children everywhere, could not understand that in middle school there was no such thing as a fair fight.

For the next three years, Boje hardly let up. Anything spherical could be lobbed at me and turned into a taunt. A little Sambo—an old-fashioned cartoonish illustration of a black boy with very dark skin, huge eyes, and big red lips—had long been used to advertise *negerboll* cookies in Sweden, and I felt a sense of dread any time I saw a boy open a package of them at lunch because I knew that the wrapper would soon be coming my way. Mats never hesitated to stand up for me.

I later learned that Mats's parents had anticipated the

racial taunts way before my own parents had and had instructed their son not to tolerate anyone picking on me. I wondered then about the boys who stood up for me and the ones who shied away from the fight. How had Team Marcus and Team Boje been formed? Was it boys who were raised right and boys who were not? Was it boys who were scared and boys who were not? The lines were split, and it wasn't about friendship. Inside the *negerboll* coliseum we were all gladiators.

CHAPTER 7

We've Got Game

Sports, in my childhood, were the great equalizer, the safe space. When skateboards came onto the scene, Mats and I practiced kick turns for hours, wiping out, racing down our driveways. We'd race everything, including bikes, although on those we preferred to pedal full speed at each other just to see what a head-on collision would feel like. (Not so great.) We hiked around the woods in our backyards, playing hours of elaborate hide-and-seek games or pretending to be mountain men or survivors from a plane wreck, desperate enough to turn to cannibalism. When we were with other kids, we dared them to skateboard down hills with no padding or shoes; we ran tennis tournaments that blocked the street, using string for a net and chalked court lines; we never stopped.

The sport we most loved was soccer. Mats and I were equally obsessed with it.

When we'd play all-kid pickup games in the neighborhood or kick balls around during school recess, the only real competition Mats and I faced was each other. Instead of that making us jealous, it made us closer. Soccer was our bond. The first non-school book I ever read was one Mats lent to me, which he'd taken out from the local library.

"Du skulle gilla den här," he said as he chucked it in my direction. You might like this.

It was the autobiography of Brazil's Edson Arantes do Nascimento, better known as Pelé, better known as the greatest soccer player in the world. I sat rock still as I read of Pelé coming to Göteborg (Göteborg!) at seventeen to play in the 1958 World Cup final. Pelé described walking onto the field of Nya Ulleví Stadium, a few miles from my house, wearing his number ten jersey: he knew the crowd was focused on him, wondering who "this skinny little black boy" was. Pelé was my first hero and my first black role model, and that book meant the world to me.

When Mats and I weren't playing soccer, we were listening to music, to whatever new singles fell into the rotation on Göteborg's pop radio station. One day, he called me over to his house to hear a new album that an older cousin had passed along, by a band called KISS. We stared at the album cover, stunned by the men in outrageous makeup, kicking up their legs, sheathed in skintight silver-and-black leather costumes. Mats held the album up to his face and pouted, just like the guys in the band.

We ran into his parents' bathroom and ransacked his

mother's makeup bag. We shouldered each other aside for the best spot in front of the mirror; Mats took the eyeliner and drew on the black star-shaped eye patch of lead singer Paul "Starchild" Stanley, while I penciled in black flames around each eye to turn myself into bassist Gene "The Demon" Simmons.

For a few months, playing KISS was definitely among our favorite pastimes. Mats was taking a woodworking class, and while the other kids made toolboxes and desk caddies, he built a wooden microphone and stand, complete with a leather "electric cord" that we could incorporate into our shows. When we wanted to perform as the whole band, we brought in other kids, but more often than not, it was just the two of us in Mats's room, listening to each of the album's nine songs in order, following along with the lyrics printed on the album sleeve. Sometimes we'd just replay our favorite, "Detroit Rock City," again and again and again. We played a lot of air guitar—Mats on lead and me on bass—and we thought Göteborg had never seen anything as fierce as us when we screamed out, "First I drink, then I smoke!" We were good Swedish boys, but we meant, when the time was right, to get into some serious trouble.

Eventually, our tastes matured, and by seventh grade, we had progressed to . . . I hate to say it . . . Sweden's own ABBA. Now, instead of wanting to strike poses, we wanted to dance. We held disco nights: we'd gather all the candy we could find and invite a dozen neighborhood girls to dance with us in Mats's basement to ABBA's latest release.

For disco night, you had to dress up. It was a little on the preppy side, though back then, we just thought we were cool. Mats and I wore knit sweaters over button-down shirts and our coolest jeans. The girls wore dresses or silky blouses and their Calvin Kleins. We only invited two or three other boys; the rest of the invitations went to girls. We wanted the odds to be in our favor.

I knew how to dance because I grew up with sisters. We danced a lot at home. Anna and Linda went to real parties, and before they'd go, they'd practice all the latest moves.

I had a crush on a girl named Anna. Same name as my sister. Mats's sister was named Anna, too. It was just a very popular name. My Anna had beautiful brown eyes and long dark hair, and she lived just a few hundred yards away from me. I liked her because she wasn't one of the loud girls in school. She was cool, but never obnoxious like some of the other "popular" girls. Anna's father worked for the city's hockey team and they went to all the games. Their car had the team's logo on it. I had no idea what her father did. He could've swept the stadium, for all I knew. He was associated with a professional team, and that made him a big shot to me.

I decided that I would tell Anna how I felt at one of our disco nights. Michael Jackson was singing "Billie Jean" as Mats's mother worked the turntable. I asked Anna if she would be my girl, and she agreed. Which meant that when a slow song came on, such as Donna Summer's "Last Dance," I could put my arm around her and hold her close. Heaven.

Back then, being boyfriend and girlfriend didn't mean a lot of one-on-one time together. Anna and I mostly hung out with Mats and his girlfriend, Ulrika. We were all twelve years old. I was so afraid of Anna's mother that I never rang her doorbell. Instead, I threw little pebbles at Anna's bedroom window to see if she could come hang out. But half the fun of going to Anna's was getting there, jumping over fences and cutting through the neighbors' backyards.

For the fourteen years that we lived in the neighborhood of Skattkärr, until I left Sweden for good, Mats and I spoke to or saw each other ninety-nine out of any one hundred days. In our minds, we ruled the neighborhood; and since we were in the same class and went to the same school, we ruled there, too.

~·~

In Sweden, if you're serious about a sport, you don't waste your time with a school team; you join a club. The club teams in Sweden operate like a farm system for the pro leagues, and going pro was all Mats and I ever thought about. By the time we were eleven, we had outgrown the small neighborhood team we played for. We both tried out and were both accepted into GAIS, Gothenburg Athletics and Sports Association, one of the city's leading club teams. GAIS was Sweden's answer to Manchester United, and its fans, including Mats's dad, were legendary in their devotion. To be accepted into their youth program was a huge deal. It meant you had a shot at joining the team.

For the next four years, Mats and I lugged our bags to the practice field every day after school and every weekend, making the five-mile trek by bus, by tram, with our moms, or in the backseat of my dad's rattly old Volkswagen Beetle. And when we took the tram, we never waited for it to pull up to our stop. We always jumped out early and ran the four blocks to the stadium, where our teammates were waiting.

Until I joined GAIS, I was used to being the only outsider in any given room. At school, diversity took the form of one Finnish kid and one Indian girl, who, like me, had been adopted young and spoke Swedish without an accent. But in GAIS, only six of the twenty-two team members were Swedish, and almost all of them were from working-class homes. All of a sudden, I had friends from Yugoslavia, Turkey, Latvia, and Finland, friends who were named not Gunnar and Sven but Mario and Tibor, friends with darker skin and darker hair. From my new teammates, I learned to speak a patois that blended foreign words with abbreviated Swedish sayings. Instead of saying *"Vad hanner anners?"*—What's going on?—we'd say *"Anners?"* To get someone's attention, we would say *"yalla,"* which meant "faster" in Arabic. And if we made a mistake, we used the English word *sorry.* It was, by our parents' standards, a lazy and improper way of speaking. To us, it was the epitome of cool.

My new teammates—even the white Swedes—all called themselves *blatte,* a historically derogatory term for immigrants that my generation claimed with pride. *Blatte* meant someone who was "dark" but, more, someone who was an outsider. It wasn't quite as charged as the term *nigga* that was favored among hip-hop-loving black people, but it was a term that made liberal-minded Swedes deeply uncomfortable. I liked that *blatte* covered everyone from displaced Ugandan Indians to former Yugoslavians to someone like me.

Unlike some of my team members, I'd been adopted as a toddler. Culturally and linguistically, I was Swedish. But the older I got, the more I could feel people respond to me as a young black man instead of a cute little black kid. The subtle shift in the body language of strangers was something I never discussed with my parents, my sisters, or even Mats. But it was lucky for me that this deepening racial awareness happened at the same time I joined GAIS. While I was beginning to sense the ways that I didn't fully belong to Swedish society, I had found a place and a group of people with whom I felt very much at home.

After practice, my teammates and I usually walked over to McDonald's, which was still relatively new in our city, and gorged on junk food. We were fascinated by how American it all seemed. Some of my school friends had gotten part-time jobs working the grill and fryers, and by the time I was in eighth grade, I decided I wanted to work at McDonald's, too. Why not get paid to be where I was hanging out every day anyway?

One day before practice, I went in and asked for an application. When I had finished it, the kid behind the counter pointed me in the direction of his manager, who couldn't have been older than twenty-one. I handed over my form, smiling and standing up straight the way my mother had taught me.

The manager held my application like something he'd picked up off the floor, touching it with only his thumb and his index finger.

"I'll let you know," he said.

I knew then and there I was not going to get a call. He

hadn't actually said anything racist, but I ricocheted, as I so often did in those teenage years, between trusting my gut and being afraid that I'd misread the entire situation. I walked out of the restaurant, not sure whether I wanted to cry or hit someone.

At practice the next day, when I told my teammates what had happened, they laughed. They thought the very notion of me, a black kid, applying to work at a place like McDonald's, was hysterical.

"You applied *where?*" my teammates asked, incredulous.

"Of course you didn't get a job!" they said. "Have you ever seen a *blatte* behind a McDonald's counter?"

At home, when I told my mother about the way the manager treated me, she did what mothers do: she offered to fight my battles for me. "I'll call him right now," she said. "He can't get away with that kind of treatment."

"No, no, please," I insisted. "I'll work somewhere else. I'll work somewhere better."

"Bry dig inte om honom," my father said. Ignore them.

The incident at McDonald's signaled to my father that it was time for him to start arming me with the history and the sense of self I would need to overcome all the slights that were sure to come my way. As a geologist, as an academic, my father believed that knowledge really was power, so he brought me books such as *The Autobiography of Malcolm X* and *Roots.* I loved those books, but I also found an even greater solace in music, and I added music, especially rap, to my race curriculum. I spent hours listening to Tupac and Public Enemy.

The first time I came to America was through playing

soccer. Our team stayed at a hotel in Times Square. We were fifteen kids and three coaches, and we were in the hotel for all of five minutes before we went running into Times Square. We must have been quite a sight, dressed all alike in our Adidas tracksuits. It was late at night and this was the mideighties, so the city wasn't as safe as it is now. But what was really amazing was that we hadn't walked a block when we ran into a rap group shooting a music video. The group was Eric B. and Rakim, and LL Cool J was making a cameo. I remember thinking, "Oh my God, we just watched them on MTV, and here they are in Times Square." It was like someone had laid out a map of my future: become a famous soccer player, travel all around the world, hang out with cool rap musicians while they shoot their music videos.

Our team's green-and-black-striped jersey earned us the nickname "the Mackerels," and I wore that jersey, and that nickname, with an unbelievable amount of pride. I like to tell people that my hometown, Göteborg, or Gburg, is like Pittsburgh by the sea. For me, wearing that jersey was like being on the kids' version of the Steelers: it said I belonged in Gburg, even if my skin said I didn't.

A few years after Mats and I joined, the adult GAIS division signed its first black player, a Tunisian midfielder named Samir Bakaou. Bakaou was not olive-skinned, like so many North Africans; he was as black as I was, and he made a point, whenever our paths would cross, of acknowledging me. He was a cool dude, never stressed on the field, always in control. The only other black males I ever saw were on TV— Carl Lewis, Michael Jackson, Desmond Tutu. They were all so far away. But Samir Bakaou trained where we trained. We didn't speak the same languages—I spoke Swedish and English, and he spoke Arabic and French—but he always nodded or winked at me, gestures that assured me that we were connected. Along with Pelé, Bakaou immediately joined the pantheon of my black male role models.

The Mackerels were good—better than good. We traveled all over Northern Europe during the seven-month season: up to Stockholm and over to Denmark, Holland, England, and Yugoslavia. We practiced two hours a day: dribbling, passing, jumping, shooting, and running wind sprints, blasting at top speed across our half of the practice field, touching the center line, then an end line and back again as many times as we could in five-minute intervals. When the coach's whistle finally blew, we fell down onto the ground wherever we were, sucking wind. Lying there with that feeling of having gone full out, staring up at the sky, blood and adrenaline pulsing through my body—I lived for that sensation.

In terms of philosophy, our coach, Lars, was influenced by the Brazilians—masters of the passing game. While many of the youth teams played one strategy—pass to the fastest guy and hope he can score—our coach wanted us to play with a mix of precision and poetry. Lars was just as proud of a fifty-yard sideline pass or of a perfectly executed cross as he was of any goals we scored. What he wanted to see on the field, the skills he taught us that are with me to this day, was the control and finesse that make soccer both a joy to play and a joy to watch.

"I'd rather you lose than win ugly," Lars said.

We weren't the top team in the league, but we won more than we lost. Mats played center defender and I was center midfield, which made me the link between offense and defense. Lars typically put us both in his starting lineup, although we were on the young side. In our first year on GAIS, we were playing against boys who were three or four years older—which only added to the thrill whenever we were lucky enough to win.

By our second year on the team, scouts had begun to appear on the sideline, looking for talent they might siphon off for their semipro adult divisions or the all-out pro teams. When a sixteen-year-old Finnish boy we often played against got scooped up for his club's pro team and became his team's high scorer, we all dreamed of following his lead. I practiced harder than ever, and for the first time, I felt a pull between wanting to do the best for the team and wanting to stand out enough to be noticed.

I knew I was good, and with each winning match, it became easier to envision a life in soccer, with GAIS as a launching pad to a pro career. I practiced every hour that I wasn't doing homework or chores. I honed every move, not just my own. I borrowed the latest soccer magazines from Mats (my father believed in only newspapers and proper books), and alone in my room, I devoured them.

In those days, there were three posters on my bedroom wall: Michael Jackson, the king and queen of Sweden (thanks, Mom), and Pelé, the man who changed the game. I spent hours imagining myself on the field as a little Pelé, dribbling down fields in Barcelona and London, outmaneuvering world-class players as I drove to the goal, winning the World

Cup with a header that would be played and replayed in slow motion on sports channels for years to come. Soccer was going to be more than my career. It would be the thing that got me out of Gburg. With soccer, I would get to see the world.

⟪⟫

By the time I turned sixteen, I had been on GAIS for four years. My life had taken on a steady, comforting routine: seven months of soccer, three months of school in which I would spend the majority of my time thinking about soccer, and two summer months in Smögen, fishing with my dad and my uncles, practicing my moves, seeing the green-and-black GAIS jersey in the scales of every beautiful fish.

At the start of our fifth season, Mats and I went down to Valhalla to see the new team roster posted on the wall outside the coach's office. We wanted to suss out the competition: who the new kids were, who might be competing for our spots in the starting lineup. We were also looking to see whom the coach had axed: we wished nothing but the worst for the lazy bums who were finally getting their comeuppance for skipping one too many practices.

We looked at the list. There was *Carestam*, up toward the top of the alphabetized page. Mats made it. But when we got to the S's, there was no *Samuelsson*. I looked again. Not there. My brain refused to process what was clearly visible in front of me. For a few moments, I just kept looking at the list, reciting the alphabet in my head. *Q, R, S, T. Where was I?* My name wasn't there, no matter how many times I looked. It sounds melodramatic to say it, but I simply

61

couldn't imagine that there was no place for me on this team, with my friends, in the game that was my world.

I slammed my fist into the bulletin board as Mats stood by, toeing the ground with a tip of one sneaker, averting his eyes.

"Javla skit!" I screamed. *"Skit! Skit! Skit!"* The four-letter word that I screamed out could hardly express the pain that I felt as my life's dream—playing soccer professionally—evaporated before my eyes.

The office door opened, and Coach Lars stuck his head out to see what was up.

"Come inside, Samuelsson," he said. "Carestam, wait here."

I followed Lars into his office, and he shut the door behind me. I sank into the chair across from his desk, which was scattered with the playbooks and lineups and photocopied schedules that represented all that had been taken away from me. I took deep breaths and tried to keep my hands from trembling.

"Marcus," he said, "I know this is disappointing. You're a great player, but you're too small. The other sixteen-year-olds outweigh you by forty or fifty pounds, some of them more. You should keep playing, but it can't be with us. Sorry."

It was the first time in my life that I had ever been fired, and I didn't even see it coming. I worked hard, I didn't flaunt the rules, I was diligent, I was disciplined, I was *good*. I was also out. Cut from the team. The only career path I'd ever considered for myself was now closed.

Although I would continue to play soccer in a smaller, lesser league, even working with a special coach to bridge that size and strength gap, eventually I had to let the dream go. And when I did, food entered my life fully.

Maybe one of the reasons that I come so hard in the food game is that I've been cut once before. I know what it's like to see your name on the list year after year, and I know the heartbreak that comes the day you look up and your name is no longer on that list. Even now, all these years after GAIS let me go, I sometimes think of myself more as a failed soccer player than an accomplished chef.

PART TWO

MY

PLAN B

CHAPTER 8

All Chips on Food

With a soccer career off the table, I decided to apply to a vocational high school. Sweden's school system was compulsory only until ninth grade, at which point many kids went on to two or three more years of gymnasium, specialized high schools meant to equip you for either a job or university.

As I considered my options, I began to play around with the idea of being a chef. Cooking was something I loved and was good at. At fifteen, I applied for and was accepted into Ester Mosesson, a school where creative types from all over Gburg studied subjects such as cooking, fashion, and graphic design.

I had never excelled in academics the way my father had, so here was a curriculum that I could finally get

67

excited about. My only formal classes were in Swedish and English—I loved languages, so that was always fun. There was a mandatory PE program, which consisted mostly of easy soccer scrimmages—again, fun. The rest of the day was spent cooking. By this point, I'd been around food and cooking for so long that I couldn't remember *not* knowing my way around a kitchen. I walked into the class feeling more than confident. On the third day, one of our instructors was running through basic knife skills for prepping vegetables. "Soon enough," he promised, "you'll dream about chopping onions."

The teacher's pattern was to demonstrate—from julienne (which is when you cut an item, such as vegetables, into small strips like matches) to chiffonade (which is when you shred a leafy vegetable like a garnish)—then have a student take his place at the cutting board and attempt to imitate. I held back at first, curious to see how much experience my new classmates had. Even under close supervision, blood was drawn. The kitchen, we quickly learned, was no place for the clumsy or distracted.

After a brief demonstration of how to cut a classic batonnet—a squared-off, oversize matchstick—a kid named Martin got a turn at the chopping board. The teacher handed over his knife, and Martin said nothing. He just took the knife and, in one fluid motion, topped and tailed the potato, cutting off the rounded ends and edges so that he had a rectangular block. He sliced the block into quarter-inch-thick slabs, then stacked the slabs in piles of three and sliced them again, lengthwise.

The group fell silent, admiring the perfectly uniform pile

of potato sticks. Martin took a towel from a peg below the counter and wiped down the knife blade.

"Did everybody see that?" our teacher asked.

My grandmother had been such a thorough and patient teacher that I came into school with basic techniques, far beyond most of the kids in my class. I knew how to hold a knife. I knew how to fillet a fish. I knew how to sauté meat in a cast-iron pan over high heat to produce a nice crust. But I could see in that mound of potatoes that Martin knew everything I knew, and more. Cooking was incorporated into his body like pure muscle memory, the same way I dribbled a soccer ball, the way the rest of us walked and breathed. From that day on, I saw that there were only two students in the entire school—me and Martin. He was the one to beat and I was the one to do it.

One of our instructors was a young Brit named John Morris. His job was to teach us how to grill, fry, sauté, and poach, all using French techniques and terminology, of course. Unlike most of our other teachers, he insisted we call him Chef John, as if we were in a professional kitchen. Chef John spoke in Swenglish, starting each class in polite Swedish and gradually slipping, as the day ground on, into a string of English curse words. He'd started off in his hometown pub, cleaning chickens and cooking liver. Then he moved to London and worked in the kitchen of the opulent Dorchester hotel, where he was promoted to *chef de partie* and cooked for the likes of Queen Elizabeth and Jimmy Carter. If he hadn't met a Swedish woman in a bar, he said, he'd still be there. But that woman had become his wife, and love had led him to Gburg.

Chef John did not have an easy task. Try demonstrating the difference between simmering and poaching on an old government-issue stove whose gas line delivered its fuel in uneven hiccups. In a professional kitchen, if a pot burns one too many times, you throw it away. At Mosesson, if teachers had discarded every utensil that had been burned one too many times, we'd have had nothing left.

Chef John's biggest obstacles, however, were his students.

"How do you know if the oil is the right temperature?" a kid named Niklas asked, interrupting Chef John's lesson on deep-frying. It was a straightforward question, but Niklas was the type of entitled kid who thought he was funnier than he actually was. I could tell by the smirk on his face that he was up to something.

Chef John answered him straight. "There are three ways to tell. One, drop in a couple of test fries. If they float up to the surface and start to bubble, and if you can hear a sizzle, then the oil's hot."

"I don't want to lose a fry," Niklas moaned dramatically. "I looooove my fries."

A few scattered snickers rippled through the room.

"The second way is to simply watch the time," Chef John continued. "If you give it about fifteen minutes, it will prob-ably be up to temperature."

Then he turned to Niklas, who stood on the other side of the vat of hot oil. "Of course, you can always put your bloody finger in the fryer."

Niklas, being more moron than comedian, chose this method. His finger wasn't in the fryer for more than a sec-ond before he began screaming, a shocked look on his face as if he hadn't actually expected it to hurt. Chef John was screaming, too. "You stupid f***ing bastard!" he said. "Why the hell did you put your f***ing finger in there? *Have you lost your mind?*"

Niklas quit the program a couple of months later, but I learned an invaluable lesson from his stupidity. The kitchen is a dangerous place, and if you want to stay safe, you've not only got to watch your own back, you've got to keep your eye on all the weak links.

⌐––⊃

In any professional kitchen, the lower-ranked staff responds to any request from above with military-like respect. "Yes, chef" is what I was taught to say whether he or she asks for a side of beef or your head on a platter. Yes, chef. Yes, chef. Yes, chef. I had failed at soccer, and the failure made me humble and determined. At Mosesson, I was determined to be the best. Soon I was serving up not only classic three-course Swedish smorgasbords but also very good renditions of coq au vin, steak au poivre, and bouillabaisse.

Halfway through the first term, my class started working in the restaurant school, cooking for customers. Most of the time, our lunch menu was pure Sweden: plates of gravlax with boiled potatoes and herring in all manner of sauces—mustard and dill, cream, curry, and 1-2-3 with slivered onions. We also prepared contemporary classics like toast Skagen: a sautéed round of bread topped with shrimp salad, finished with a spoonful of whitefish roe. Dinner, on the other hand, was typically French, which was considered an elegant cut above homey Swedish fare: sole meunière or duck à l'orange.

We worked in rotating shifts, so I might be a waiter for three weeks, then a dishwasher, then a line cook. I was a decent waiter and I knew it was useful to see how customers behaved in the front of the house, how they ordered, and how they regarded their meal once it was served, but I never felt at home in the front like I did in the back. The back of the house was where the real action, the real creativity, was. Even with only forty seats in the restaurant, and even if only half of them were filled, the kitchen was guaranteed to be humming at a pitch that bordered on chaos. And it was that organized chaos that I loved. I still do.

At restaurant school, the kitchen hierarchy was structured like most professional kitchens—using the classic French *brigade de cuisine*. Each *chef de partie* was assigned a distinct task—meat, fish, salads—and one person was designated the expediter, who organized and dispensed orders as they came in from the dining room.

Although teamwork systems had been around in professional kitchens since the Middle Ages, it was the now legendary French chef Georges Auguste Escoffier who codified it and put it all down on paper at the beginning of the twentieth century in his classic book, *Le Guide Culinaire*. The success of the *brigade* depended on employees understanding and embracing two tenets: one being the hierarchy system, and two being the *chef de partie* division of labor, which compartmentalized the tasks of the kitchen into *parties* or parts, each with its own managing chef. Whatever your status, from *garçon* and *commis* at the bottom to *chef de cuisine* at the top, you had to learn where you were in the pecking order. When anyone above you asked for something, you said "Yes, chef" and double-timed it to meet his or her demands. In turn, you had the right to order around whoever fell below your rank.

In restaurant terms, an expediter is only as good as her or his ability to "order fire." This means that as the orders come in, the expediter must order the dishes so that everything will be ready to serve at once. A table of four might be having a broiled chicken, a medium steak, a rare steak, and a poached turbot fillet: each entrée would be cooked for a different amount of time and by different *chefs de partie*. The expediter calculates when to start each dish, using backward-counting math and accounting for any extra steps, like pan deglazing, a process where you pour a liquid, such as chicken stock or wine, into a pan to get the bits off the bottom after you've fried meat in the pan. The bits and liquid combine to make a delicious sauce. Or meat resting—when you cook meat in a pot or grill, the juices go to the center. It's good to let the meat rest afterward so the juices can move back to the edge of the meat to make it flavorful throughout. The ability to impose order on so much fire is the difference between a great restaurant and one that is merely good; the difference between a flawless service and one that has customers complaining and skimping on tips.

The meals we cooked had been copied straight out of our cooking bibles: *Larousse Gastronomique* and *The Escoffier Cookbook*. Appetizers led sensibly into main courses, and side dishes counterpointed or complemented entrées, but nothing about them seemed exciting or surprising or fresh. Every day I would look at the menu and wonder, What if we paired the duck à l'orange with curried fried rice instead of serving it with the traditional potatoes dauphinoise? If thyme and mustard added such wonderful flavors to the roasted lamb gigot, couldn't we do a similar variation with roasted goat instead? The desire to mix cultures and foods was already in me. But this wasn't just about my desire to introduce international flavors into traditional cuisine. I could also see that at the school, we prized French food above our own national culinary treasures. I learned more about the foods of the Alsace in France than I did about Västerbotten, the Swedish county that produced the country's best cheese. Soon, that would begin to change.

CHAPTER 9

Earning My Knives

People went out all the time in Göteborg, but not to eat. They might meet for a beer after work or to watch soccer together at a bar, but food was never the center of socializing, the way it is in cities like Barcelona or Paris, where people live their lives in restaurants. Gburg's blue-collar roots fed into this eat-at-home lifestyle. Factory workers had neither the time nor the disposable income to waste an evening over a leisurely meal. In truth, it wasn't just about time or money: as a whole, Sweden was way behind the curve on fine dining. It wasn't until the mid-1980s, when I was starting culinary school, that the first Swedish restaurants, Eriks Fiks and L'Escargot in Stockholm, received their first Michelin stars, the prestigious European ratings system that designates the best restaurants in Europe.

Despite the training ground of the forty-seat restaurant, Mosesson really groomed its students for institutional placements such as hospital and school cafeterias. Practically speaking, there was no local restaurant scene to provide jobs for the graduates, even if the students wanted to stay in town. The result was an environment that didn't foster much creativity or competition among those of us who had chosen to cook for a living. There were no customers to build a relationship with; the only people willing to pay for haute cuisine were foreigners and corporate diners with expense accounts, neither of whom offered the steady, loyal patronage that restaurants count on to survive. Without a fine-dining culture, it's difficult to develop a palate that extends beyond whatever it is your family serves you.

My own family ate out two or three times a year, tops. We'd go out to celebrate the big events, like Anna getting into a selective school, Dad earning his PhD, or Linda landing a job at a record company. Eventually, my father decided that we'd eat only foreign food when we went out because my mother would find any Swedish meal we were served in a restaurant lacking and, thus, would have a hard time enjoying herself. "Helga could do this better," she would sniff, disappointed. And, probably because of its familiarity, Swedish food was never worth the price. "Look at what this costs!" she'd say, pushing the menu away.

The ultimate luxury for most of the people we knew was peel-and-eat shrimp. Most of the shellfish in the area had been caught in my father's hometown, Smögen, where it was boiled right on the boat, trucked down to Göteborg, and served with white toast, mayonnaise, and lemon. Peel-and-eat shrimp was popular because of the method of eating it. Proper table manners in Swedish homes required the use of a fork and a knife for everything, from fruit to sandwiches, but peel-and-eat was a vacation from all that buttoned-up propriety. The shrimp came out on a big platter, pink and plump, with the heads still on, and each person took a handful to his or her plate. From there, you would peel about ten at a time, then dip your hands in a bowl of water to clean them off. Next, you smeared a piece of toast with the mayo, arranged your peeled shrimp on top, and finished it with a sprinkle of chopped dill and a squeeze of lemon. Once you were done, you'd start the routine all over again. It was that tasty.

Everyone in Gburg grew up on peel-and-eat, but my family had it more often than most because of my father's Smögen heritage. Dad taught my sisters and me how to eat shrimp properly, sucking the meat out of the head, much the same way that people from New Orleans eat their mudbugs at a crawfish boil. My mother, Skånsan that she was, had a hard time adapting my father's approach. She stuck to the tail meat instead.

Decades later, when I met one of my most treasured mentors, the legendary New Orleans chef Leah Chase, I know that the way I attacked her crawfish was one of the reasons that she took a liking to me. I wasn't just an African-born/European-raised chef with a big profile and a big head full of highfalutin ideas. No, ma'am. Leah Chase saw me eat and knew that I was a brown-skinned boy who loved good food and also knew better than to waste any of it.

By the time my second year at Mosesson rolled around, my ambition for food was such that the curriculum seemed not only limited, but also a waste of time. I didn't know where I would end up or what I would cook, but I had a vague sense there was a world of amazing restaurants outside Göteborg. Without classmates or professors to push me or encourage my dreaming, I feared I would become complacent. We continued to focus on the basic skills, everything from butchering to food-handling safety, and to split our time between lectures and hands-on practice. It was as if we were in junior high, not culinary school.

To keep myself sharp, I turned each exercise into a little contest. Could I fill the pastry shells faster than any of my classmates? Could I wash and chop that dill faster than the teacher? Could I finish each squirt of whipped cream with the exact same curl?

A few weeks into my second year, it was clear that I'd outgrown what the school had to offer. But if I left before the program was over, my father's disappointment would be too much to bear. I'd already decided not to go to university, a big blow for Dad, a man with a doctorate and a deep belief in higher education. If I dropped out of culinary school, even if I dropped out because I wanted something more challenging, my father would see me as a quitter and see any future success as accidental, instead of being the result of the two things he valued most: focus and discipline. The only way out, as I saw it, was an off-site internship in a real restaurant. They came up frequently and were listed on a board at my school. For the next few months, every time I saw a new listing, I applied. Every time, I got no further than I had when I submitted my application to work at McDonald's. Until Tidbloms.

Tidbloms was housed in a stately brick Victorian that dated back to 1897, when it had served as a dormitory for Scottish craftsmen who came to work at a nearby lumber mill. Over the years, it had gone through tough times, operating as a warehouse, then a flophouse, then a deli. When I came along, it had just been renovated into a charming inn, and the restaurant had been made over accordingly.

I walked through the dining room and into the kitchen, where a shaggy-haired young guy, probably in his mid-twenties, was picking through a tub of oysters, smelling some, knocking on some others with his knuckle, and cocking his head to listen for something.

"These are good," he said to another young guy standing next to him. "You can accept the delivery."

The guy said nothing, but turned and hustled toward the kitchen's back door. I introduced myself. "I'm looking for the chef," I said.

"I'm the chef," he said. "I'm Jorgen. How can I help you?"

Every bit of buzz I'd heard about Tidbloms centered on what Jorgen had done in its kitchen. How he'd assembled a strong team of cooks, and how consistently he turned out high-quality food, a blend of Swedish ingredients with the sauces and attitudes of French cuisine.

Dinner, I was told, was when the best ingredients came out: the morels, the cherry tomatoes, the fresh basil and tarragon. I wanted to be around this higher class of food, but

I also sensed a seriousness about the work that would be an antidote to what I was getting at school. Even though late afternoon was the slow prep period, with no customers in the front of the house, no one seemed to be slacking off. Even the porter who brought in the oysters did his job as if a fire were lit under him.

"I'll work hard," I promised Jorgen after detailing my Mosesson studies and summer jobs. He agreed to give me a four-week internship. I was sixteen years old.

What a relief it was to work in a real kitchen, serving real food made by real cooks to real paying customers. I was assigned the most basic of tasks, just above dishwasher, but from my first shift, working side by side with a professional restaurant staff, I felt the camaraderie and effort I had known on the soccer field. I turned on the plate warmer at precisely eleven o'clock each morning. I stocked the walk-in refrigerator as soon as the chef cleared each delivery. I set up the station for the *saucier*, replenishing his *mise en place* so that he could fill any order during meal service without having to hunt down an ingredient and chop it. I did more than peel potatoes by the hundreds; I washed them, peeled them, and tournéed them, cutting them into identical shapes, two inches long with seven equally wide sides. For this task, one of the cooks would lend me his own tourné knife—real cooks own their own sets of knives, which they carry in long, soft cases, and the tourné has a curved blade that looks like a bird beak, the name often used to describe it. I was always careful to wipe down the blade and handle before giving it back, another sign of care and respect. There might have been clear lines of status in the hierarchy of the kitchen, but we had a common goal, and everyone understood that his contributions mattered.

Bengt, one of Tidbloms's cooks, lived near my parents and gave me a ride home whenever we worked the same shifts. As we puttered along the E20 highway, we talked about our plans to conquer the cooking world.

"My next step," he announced one night, "will be to work for Leif and Crister." Leif Mannerström and Crister Svantesson often worked as a team and were currently helming La Scala, Göteborg's most upscale eatery.

I had a little trouble swallowing Bengt's confident pronouncement and let him know. He was competent, but I didn't think he was *that* good.

"Listen," he said, ignoring my lack of enthusiasm, "if you do well at Tidbloms, if you impress them, I'll see what I can do about getting you into La Scala down the line, too." He didn't even have his own job yet, but he was promising to bring *me* along? I would soon find that this was the way among chefs and their tribes: you follow a great chef anywhere he might go.

I learned something with every shift. My first week, I learned how a proper fish stock was made. Where my grandmother threw a mishmash of bones into a pot with water and chopped red onions, mixing salmon and haddock and letting it cook at a furious boil, Tidbloms used only finer, more delicate fish, like turbot and sole. The chefs added fresh parsley, peppercorns, white wine, and the green part of the leek, cooking it slowly, barely simmering, coaxing out flavors rather than bludgeoning them. I learned how to fillet fish faster and without wasting any flesh. I learned how to slice just under the tough, pearly silver skin when cleaning a tenderloin of beef so that I could pull it away from the bone more easily, and how much simpler it was to fillet a tenderloin than a rack of lamb. Most of all, I learned what it meant to never gear down, to work with a constant sense of purpose. In school, we'd do only one thing at a time: Today, we're going to make whipped cream. Today, we're going to make veal stock. At Tidbloms, everyone had five things on his plate, and all of them needed to be done immediately.

After four weeks, when my time at Tidbloms was just about up, I couldn't bear the thought of going back to Mosesson full-time. I went to see Jorgen between lunch and dinner services. He had no office, so any clean stretch of counter could become his desk. He was writing out a menu for the next week. I waited for him to notice me, but his head remained bent over his task. I cleared my throat, and he looked up.

"Hey, Marcus. What's going on?" Jorgen asked.

I was so afraid of him saying no that the plan I'd hatched came tumbling out in one nonstop flood: "Chef, I can't go back to that rinky-dink school restaurant when I could be here working with you. I have to do a certain number of hands-on cooking hours for school, and if I did all my cooking hours for free here at Tidbloms, do you think you'd be able to sign for them so I can get school credit? You'd have to let my cooking teacher know it's okay with you and then sign off on my hours at the end of each reporting period. I can give you the guy's number, and if there are any forms,

I'll get them from the school. You don't have to do anything extra besides letting me stay." I took a breath. "What do you think?"

Jorgen smiled. "Why didn't you ask sooner?" he said.

With the placement figured out, I took the idea back to my cooking teacher.

"Why should we make an exception for you?" he asked. "This is not standard policy."

I responded with the confidence of a cocky teenager. Or the desperate. "You know I'm going to become a real cook when I leave here," I said. "Unlike most of the kids here, I'm serious about it. And if I don't get more real-world experience, I'll fall behind in my chances of getting a good job after I graduate. Please?"

"Okay, Samuelsson, we'll give it a try," he said. "But you can't miss any of your other classes. Remember: you're still in school."

⌁

When I arrived in Sweden, I was assigned a birthday of November 11. Each year, on that day, my mother or grandmother baked a cake, and at the end of supper, I opened a handful of presents. My grandmother gave me sweaters she'd knitted herself; my father gave me books; and my mother gave me clothes she thought I needed, usually more stylish than I would have picked out on my own. I could count on Linda and Anna to go in together on something cool. The year before, they'd cooked up the perfect Afro-Swedish gift: a Public Enemy album and a pair of turquoise Converse high-tops.

That year—my seventeenth birthday—as my mother cleared the cake plates from the kitchen table, Anna leaned over to Linda and whispered something in her ear. Linda sprang up from her chair and ran downstairs to Anna's room. She was back a minute later with a long rectangular box wrapped in paper I recognized from the previous Christmas.

"Open it," Anna said.

I took my time peeling the tape off. The box seemed awfully similar to the ones we gave my father on his birthday, the ones that held ties he promptly wore to the office for the next week straight and then buried in the sock drawer of his closet. With the paper off, I could see it was a box from Holmens Herr, the classiest—and least cool—menswear store in town. I tried to mask my disappointment and lifted the lid, psyching myself up to show them only happiness.

It was not a tie. It was a brand-new cook's knife with an eight-inch-long carbon-steel blade. This was the multipurpose knife every chef needs, with a blade thin enough to chop herbs, but a wide flat surface for crushing or picking up food. Better still, it was the Rolls-Royce of knives, brandwise, made by the French company Sabatier.

"I don't know what to say," I said, and when I hugged them, I meant it.

⌒⌒⊃

I worked at Tidbloms every day for the rest of the year, which made school bearable. My father might have known next to nothing about fine dining, but he had ingrained in me a flawless work ethic: I knew to show up on time, to listen to instructions, and never to talk back to my bosses.

And the hard work paid off. I might have lost my place on the soccer team because I wasn't as big as the rest of the guys, but in the kitchen, my size didn't matter. All that mattered was the work.

The cooks thanked me by letting me do more than simple prep work; I began to make *à la minute* sauces—those we cooked to order. For sole meunière, I'd step in after the fish had been cooked in butter, then add a few more tablespoons to the pan and watch until it turned golden brown. I stirred in some minced parsley and poured in lemon juice, then took a half-teaspoon taste of it to see if it needed salt. Once I got it right, I handed the pan back to the cook, who checked my flavoring and drizzled the sauce over the plated fish.

At Tidbloms, I learned the danger of complacency. Dialing it in is one of a chef's worst habits. No matter how tired you are, no matter how stressed, you can't take shortcuts. One day, we were serving a broiled cod special. I was helping out at the fish station and doing some of the final seasoning adjustments with salt and pepper. After half a dozen orders went out onto the floor, I had my seasoning down pat. The next day, I helped out at the fish station again, and I performed the same final role of seasoning the daily special. All seemed to be going well until Jorgen passed by and saw me shaking salt onto the plate.

He came over and took a taste of what I'd been working on.

He spit it into a napkin. "What the hell is this?" he asked. Turns out I'd been salting gravlax, a salt-cured fish.

He was furious—wasting good food was a no-no—and I thought I'd be fired. I felt sick. But he didn't fire me. My mistake was one of judgment, not of laziness, and to him, the difference between those mattered.

I redeemed myself by working harder and faster than I ever had before. That was the pace of Tidbloms all the time—guys cooking six things at once with a constant sense of urgency but never panic. If we had an unusually busy lunch service, Jorgen would ask me to stay on beyond my scheduled shift, and I always said yes. "Yes, chef" is such a common parlance in a professional kitchen. You don't even have to think about it for your mouth to form the words. You get asked to do something and you say yes. "Yes, chef" were the first words out of my mouth each morning and the last words I uttered as I left the restaurant each night. "Good night, Marcus," Jorgen would call out. I wouldn't say, "Have a good night, too." I'd say, "Yes, chef." I didn't want to miss any chance I got to see the world that was opening up before me.

No matter how much I learned at Tidbloms, I never caught up with my classmate Martin back at Mosesson. The day we graduated, he won the school's top honors. Martin was too nice a guy to resent, but there was another difference between us that kept me from feeling a twinge of envy. Since the age of twelve, Martin had worked in his family's catering business. While we were at Mosesson, he continued to work for his dad in his off-school hours, and when a big job came in, he'd miss out on a few days of school. I envied Martin's proficiency and talent, but I did not envy that his fate was sealed. He would eventually step into his father's shoes, take over the family business, and never leave Göteborg. Maybe he could live with that, but the mere thought made me feel like the walls around me were closing in.

I graduated second in our class and walked away with a handshake from the principal, a diploma, and my first full set of knives, carbon steel blades and riveted wood handles, each blade's weight counterbalanced by the tang, a strip of metal that continued through to the end of the handle. I would cherish those knives for years. They were the one constant in my luggage, along with my journals, as I made my way from country to country, continent to continent.

CHAPTER 10

Belle Avenue

In the winter of 1989, when I walked through Belle Avenue's doors as its newest *köksnisse*, or kitchen boy, it was probably one of the top five restaurants in Sweden. In the front of the house, three layers of white linen covered each of the room's fifty tables. Leather banquettes ringed the room. Knowledgeable, seasoned waiters were never more than a few steps away. A sommelier with a sterling silver tastevin around his neck stood by the bar, ready to guide guests through the extensive French wine list. A tastevin, which looks like a cup, is used to taste the wine—just a tiny splash—before it is poured. This is to ensure the wine is not flawed in any way. The room operated at a muffled murmur as if both servers and patrons had agreed to treat the chef, and the meals he created, with the same deference one might show a great opera singer.

Attached to the main dining room was a kitchen that served more than just the restaurant. It fed all of the Park Avenue Hotel, including its bar and grill, a dinner theater with singing waiters, room service, and three banquet halls on the mezzanine floor. From sunrise to midnight, there was hardly a minute of downtime for the staff, fifty men and also a few women scattered in the traditional female kitchen roles of salad-making and pastry. Women did not have it easy in kitchens. I came in at the level of *köksnissen;* the only ones who ranked below me were the *garçons* and the interns, young guys who worked in the basement doing thankless prep work and cleanup. On my first day, I was issued my first chef's jacket and houndstooth kitchen pants and told to report immediately to the fish department.

Gordon was my boss. He was a fortysomething former rugby player from Australia who seemed to have a perpetual sunburn, even in winter. He was the *boucher,* the butcher, and his job was to process all the meat and fish when it came into the kitchen. Gordon was physically powerful, with a personality to match. He was quick to laugh at a joke, but he didn't hesitate to shut you down if you were wasting time.

My main tasks were to unload fish orders and keep the refrigerator clean. The box, as we called the walk-in refrigerator, was lined with shelves and had four tall rolling trolleys in its center. Keeping it clean was the most physically difficult job I've ever had in a kitchen, not just because the fish came packed tight in large, cumbersome crates, but also because I had to haul hundreds of pounds of ice each shift to keep it from spoiling. You knew you'd done the job right if you didn't smell anything when you walked into the box; even fish that had been in-house for two or three days shouldn't give off the slightest odor.

I started every morning at six o'clock. I emptied out each shelf and trolley, transferring the fish temporarily to the produce refrigerator. I poured hot water over each shelf to melt any stray ice, then wiped it down with a diluted bleach solution. I scrubbed the floor with a steel scrubber, and refilled the à la carte trolley with the fish that had been butchered for that day, so cooks could come and grab what they needed as soon as it had been ordered. Deep plastic bins filled the shelves along the wall. They, too, needed to be wiped out and re-iced, and they held some of the longer-storage items, like the caviars and roes; the crabs, lobsters, and shrimp; the gravlax and smoked salmon. By ten a.m., my time in the box was done.

Between lunch and dinner, I restocked the fish station's *mise en place*, which meant chopping, shredding, and slicing every herb, condiment, and flavoring ingredient the chef would need during his shift, and putting each one into small plastic containers that lined the perimeter of his counter work space. In Sweden, dill was a principal seasoning, but chives, fennel, and other spices were also important.

In the beginning, I couldn't see past my mountain of tasks to absorb the approach and creativity of the lead chefs, but I tasted the food and saved the menus. Antlow, an older chef, didn't make fun of my naive questions. He was old enough to be my father; maybe he saw me as a son rather than a competitor. When I was working with him on an

Marcus, age five, stops to pick flowers on a family hike through the countryside (1975). *Collection of the author*

Marcus and his mother, Anne Marie, enjoy the sun during a lakeside picnic (1974). *Collection of the author*

Marcus's father, Lennart, at his fiftieth birthday party in Göteborg (1982). *Collection of the author*

The summer after his adoption, Marcus enjoys the sun in the backyard of the family's house in Göteborg (1974). *Collection of the author*

Three years after their adoption, Kassahun and Fantaye are officially baptized as Marcus and Linda Samuelsson (1976). *Collection of the author*

Marcus and his sister Linda, in their Easter Saturday outfits, outside the family's summer house in Smögen (1974). *Collection of the author*

Marcus sits on his mother's lap, next to his sisters, Anna (*middle*) and Linda (1976). *Collection of the author*

Marcus and Linda decorate buns for the holiday season in Mormor Helga's kitchen (1974). *Collection of the author*

Marcus, age twelve, in the portrait his parents had taken to announce his confirmation ceremony (1982).
Collection of the author

During the summer in Gburg, pickup games of soccer were a daily event. *From top left:* Peter, Klaus, Marcus, and Mats (1983).
Collection of the author

Marcus's adoptive mother, Anne Marie, and natural father, Tsegie, meet for the first time in Abragodana, Tsegie's village in Ethiopia (2009). *Collection of the author*

Marcus (*second from left*) with his father, half sisters, and mother, Anne Marie (2009). *Collection of the author*

Anne Marie and Tsegie stand with Marcus and his new wife, Maya, at the altar (2009). *Collection of the author*

event, he always saved a small piece of meat or a taste of a sauce for me.

He told me good cooking was something that engaged all of your senses. "You're not a shoemaker," he said. Which meant you had to know that a truffle opens up its flavors in heat, so you added your truffles to a sauce at the very end so you didn't cook them out. You checked a sauce not by looking at it, but by dipping a spoon into it and then watching how the sauce stuck to the metal. If it slid right off, the sauce was too thin; if it coated the spoon, it was ready. I tasted and learned, and I knew he was showing me purely out of generosity. I promised myself that when I became a chef, I would do that, too.

On Saturday nights, when I wasn't working, I would go to Mormor's and help prepare the big family supper. She loved to ask me questions about the kitchen at Belle Avenue as we stood at her counter, mixing cod with breadcrumbs to make fish balls. "What do you cook at Belle Avenue, Mackelille?" she asked, cracking open an egg and adding it to the fish mixture.

"I don't actually cook yet," I explained. "Mostly I chop and mop."

Ever faithful, she assured me that my time would come. "Don't worry," she said. "Soon they'll have you cooking, and they'll be sorry they waited so long."

⌐•⌐

One morning, another *köksnisse* named Jakob and I were in charge of breaking down fresh hunks of turbot for the day's lunch service. They would be used in one of my favorite dishes: braised turbot on the bone. Jakob and I were not yet cooking the dish, but we were charged with cutting eleven-pound hunks of turbot into steaks. Even with our carefully honed fillet knives, the task promised to be slow; cutting through bone was tough.

"Let's use the band saw!" Jakob said. We had seen Gordon use it to butcher dense cuts of beef and frozen fish, but never with wet, fresh fish. No matter: the first fish went through perfectly, and we thought we were in business. We did another, then another, no problem. But when Jakob got to the fourth fish, it slipped out of his grasp. The blade went through his finger instead of the fish, fully severing his fingertip. Blood spurted everywhere.

Jakob writhed on the floor, screaming in pain and holding his hand. I started shouting for help.

All the commotion brought over the executive chef, who looked down at Jakob and chimed in at the top of his lungs.

"What have you idiots done?" he screamed.

Someone, definitely not me, kept his wits about him, picked up Jakob's fingertip, dropped it into a bag of ice, and rushed him to the hospital. A few hours later, it was successfully reattached. But Jakob never came back. At the staff meal later that day, there was no mention of what had happened. The older crew knew it was stupid rookie work; the younger ones realized it could have been any one of them.

At Belle Avenue, I learned what it was like to serve a meal to guests who were in no rush at all. When people booked dinner at our restaurant, they came to spend the evening. This gave the kitchen more time to work on each dish, to replace speed as a priority with attention to detail. I started to appreciate the implications of this careful work, how differently garlic cooked depending on whether it was sliced, chopped, or crushed, how differently it released its flavor into the pan. Up until this point, fine dining had been an abstraction, a distant summit to ascend.

Now that I saw how much strategy and how many levels cooking could operate on, it was clear to me: what we did in the restaurant was not all that different from the work the museum curators did across the street. We were both, in our way, trying to engage our customers' senses, take them out of their day-to-day life, and every once in a while, when they fell in love with a really well-executed Rydberg (pan-seared beef and potatoes in a red wine sauce) or ended their meal with a sweet botrytis Sémillon, they looked at the world in a slightly new way.

In jazz, a musician who is striving for a new kind of perfect is said to have gone "deep in the shed." That's what happened to me at Belle Avenue. It went from being a gig—a highly coveted one, but a gig all the same—to being my laboratory, my studio, my church. I never left. I worked my shift as quickly as I could, but it was never about getting done so I could get out; it was so I could learn something else. I started in the fish-cleaning department, and then I went into the meat-cleaning department, then I got bumped up to junior cook on the fish station, then *commis* on the meat station. I did a turn in pastry and in *garde manger*, where we handled cold hors d'oeuvres, salads, and charcuterie. There were fifteen separate service stations in that kitchen, and I was determined to go through each one.

On my rare nights off, I met up with my friends at one of the local cafés. One night there was a group of girls at the next table, and one in particular caught my eye. She was speaking Swedish, but she didn't look Swedish; she had dark, shiny hair and almond-shaped eyes. I was never shy with girls—I have my sisters to thank for that—so I went over and introduced myself.

Carina was cute and smart and she was, like me, Swedish but not "Swedish." Her father was a Swede, but her mother was Japanese. We started dating, and quickly became a couple. I ignored the fact that she smoked cigarettes, something that I'd never done and that, as I developed into a chef, seemed like the ultimate palate killer.

Carina's family lived in a rooftop apartment in the center of town, and while most teenage boys would be happier to be alone with their girlfriends, I was secretly pleased whenever her parents were around. They represented a world outside of Gburg, and for me that glimpse of the larger world was everything. I loved Sweden, but I didn't want to stay there. I took my job at Belle Avenue so seriously because I hoped that it would lead to bigger things—in France, because all great chefs had to do a stint in France, but also in London and New York. I was interested in anybody and anything that represented the places I hadn't been but wanted to see.

Carina's father, Sven, was an architect in the city planning department, and he would talk to me about the way a city's environment can influence people's lives. Like my father, he was the first white-collar professional to come out of his family. Carina's mother, Kikoko, had a little shop in the city center, where she sold Japanese imports and foreign novelties, everything from Hello Kitty to Snoopy. Sometimes, when I'd go over to Carina's house to hang out, her mother would make us Japanese snacks. The flavors blew my mind: this food seemed to be based on an entirely different calculation of flavor, texture, and balance. The first dish I remember her offering me was a plate of cucumber spears drizzled with white miso and topped with bonito flakes. Crisp, cold vegetables, earthy fermented sauce, and delicate slivers of fish that practically melted at the touch.

From that point on, I tried to look hungry whenever Kikoko was at home. When she wasn't, Carina and I would cook together and argue about which Japanese condiments I could or couldn't use. I couldn't read the labels, of course, and even the translated ones meant nothing to me, so I was ready to taste and try everything.

⌒

Tony Bowman, the chef in charge of all hotel dining other than Belle Avenue, knew I wanted to see the world. And typically, your boss would find placement for you.

"Marcus," he said after we'd finished breaking down a banquet buffet one afternoon, "I'm going to send you to *stage* in Amsterdam."

I held off from calling my mother and telling her immediately so I could break the news to her and Dad at the same time, in person, over dinner.

"Amsterdam?" my father said. "I don't think that's such a good idea. I've traveled there for work, and I don't think they have much in the way of food. And besides, it's a very druggy society. You could fall in with the wrong element."

I appealed to my mother. "Mom," I said, "I'm not messing up. I'm not out there drinking like a lot of the guys. I work and come home and that's it. Besides, you don't have to leave Göteborg to do drugs."

Mom agreed, but Dad held firm. "If they are willing to give you Holland now, France will come in time. That's where you've always wanted to go. I think you should hold out for something better."

In one day, my whole world had come together and then, a few hours later, completely fallen apart. I didn't know enough about Amsterdam to argue with my father, and while I had never been reluctant to debate him, I felt I had to respect his wishes. After all, I still lived under his roof.

The next day, I looked at my shoes while I told Tony I couldn't go. He looked at me intensely, as if he were trying to bring my face into focus.

"I thought you were in charge of your life," he said. "You're eighteen years old now, Marcus. How come you're not in charge?"

CHAPTER 11

Switzerland

The journey to Interlaken took thirty hours. It began with a late-morning ferry from Göteborg to Denmark, during which the normally quiet boat was overtaken by boozy Danish college kids who started pounding overpriced beers from the snack counter even before the cranes of Göteborg harbor disappeared from sight. As loud as the Danes were, I fell into a dead sleep. I'd had none the night before. Mats and I had been out all night, leaving me just enough time to pack my bag just before dawn. I woke up to a staticky voice on the PA system announcing our arrival in the port town of Frederikshavn and to the gentle bump of the boat as it kissed the side of the pier.

Because I'd made this same transfer to the train station

traveling with my soccer teams many times before, and because I was still in a Scandinavian country, I felt more at home than abroad, a feeling that stayed with me all the way down through the peninsula of Jutland, until the train crossed over the border from Denmark to Germany.

I was going to Switzerland, to be a *commis* for six months at a famous resort hotel in Interlaken called Victoria Jungfrau. I was nineteen years old.

I had packed my knives—my most treasured possessions—which I'd wrapped in the leather roll my grandmother had made for me.

"Don't buy that," she'd said when she saw how much the rolls cost. She went and studied them in a store downtown, then came home and fashioned one herself, sturdier and more handsome than the cheap nylon ones she'd seen.

I wrapped the roll, my French pepper mill, and a Japanese sharpening stone Carina had given me inside the two chef's jackets that my Belle Avenue coworkers had presented to me as a going-away gift. On my last day of work, the hotel chef, Tony, had handed them to me, which seemed fitting since he was the one who had arranged the gig for me at Victoria in the first place. He'd been a *commis* there himself, ten years before.

"Don't screw this up," he told me. "I'll hear about it if you do."

My other essentials included jeans, running shoes and the turquoise Converse sneakers I wore for work, my Walkman, and a pile of fresh notepads and pens so I could write down everything I saw, learned, and tasted.

Back in Göteborg, I'd left some ends tied up more

cleanly than others. My girlfriend, Carina, didn't want to let go. When Tony made me the offer, I thought the timing was perfect. Carina had gotten an offer to model in Japan. We would both move on to the rest of our lives, I figured. It was time.

Carina saw it differently.

"I'll wait for you, then," she said when I told her about Switzerland.

"No, no," I said. "You should go to Tokyo and live with your aunt."

"No. I'll wait for you right here."

I didn't want her to wait. I didn't want to have any ties to Sweden beyond my immediate family. I was moving on.

"I don't know when I'll be back," I said.

"That's okay," she said. "I'll wait."

After a point, I stopped trying to talk to her. We were breaking up, as far as I was concerned. Cooking was the only thing I had room for. Cooking was the only thing I wanted to make room for.

There was nothing clean about my last loose end, which was the question of what I was going to do about the army. Sweden hadn't taken part in a war for the last hundred years—not officially, at least—but it maintained an army, and service was mandatory. In my father's generation, this duty was something you never questioned. In mine, and especially among my *blatte* friends who felt only marginally welcome in the country much of the time, the army seemed obsolete, a waste of time.

But once I had turned eighteen, my father started to bring up the topic every now and then.

"Don't worry about it," I'd say. "I'm not going."

This was a position my father simply couldn't understand. To him, the only reason you should be excused from military service was if you were mentally ill or physically incapacitated. I was neither, so he believed I should go and serve. I suspect, too, that he felt I was a little too close to my mother, too protected by her. Maybe my cooking even baffled him. The army would make a man out of me.

"You can do something that has nothing to do with guns," my mother suggested, trying to broker a compromise. But it wasn't the guns; it was that nothing about the army fit into my dream of becoming a chef.

CHAPTER 12

Becoming a Man

The moment the train crossed from the small town of Padborg, Denmark, into the slightly larger town of Harrislee, Germany, something broke open inside me. I felt like I was at the beginning of a new path, one I'd forged by myself. This was a job *I'd* gotten, that *I'd* earned, and for the first time in my life, I recognized the weight of adult responsibility and welcomed it. By the time I changed trains in the Hamburg station, the comforts of Scandinavia seemed fully behind me.

German was the language of business at Victoria Jungfrau, Tony had told me, and in order to keep up, I'd need to get fluent fast.

Our route took a fairly direct path south, and every couple

of hours, we'd stop in a town big enough that I recognized the name: Hannover, then Göttingen, then Darmstadt. The closer we got to Munich, the more languages I heard, and I recognized many of the tongues of my *blatte* teammates. Poles and Slavs boarded, and when I switched trains again, this time in Munich, my seatmates were a Greek family who had brought a multicourse picnic with them. They spread paper napkins across their laps and ate olives and pita bread dipped in a garlicky eggplant spread or covered with slices of feta they cut from a block with a pocketknife. I tried not to stare, but the mother must have seen me sneaking glances. She put two dark dolma rolls on a napkin and handed them to me, smiling and nodding as she pressed them into my palm.

"*Efkharistó,*" I said, using the one Greek word I'd learned from hanging out at my friend Tomas's apartment. Thank you.

The mother laughed. I'd probably butchered the word, but she seemed pleased that I would even try. I bit into the soft, fat finger of the stuffed grape leaf. I had tasted these once or twice before at a café in Gburg, but they'd always seemed too dense to me, the rice packed too tight and with little flavor beyond the tang of the leaf. These dolmas, though, were different. They were lighter. They had currants and pine nuts mixed in with the rice, a hint of fresh tomato sauce and lemon juice. They were also warm, as if they had been made that very morning. I closed my eyes and smiled to show how much I liked what I was eating, and from that point on she fed me as if I were another one of her children.

Beyond Munich, it wasn't only the passengers who were

different. The landscape had grown progressively greener—June in central Germany was certainly further along than June in Denmark, but now we were heading southwest and into the Alps. As soon as we crossed into Switzerland, the train started to climb and the mountains exploded all around us. My mother would love this, I thought. They looked just like the ones in *The Sound of Music*, one of her favorite films.

My last transfer was in Bern, where I moved from a sleek, modern train to its older, clunkier cousin, its smaller cars better equipped to make the tight turns and bends of the last twenty-five miles we had to cover in order to reach Interlaken. Once again, a new crop of people boarded the train with me. These people spoke only German, and they seemed more reserved; they were quieter and more formal in their interactions with each other, even when they were obviously family. There were still picnics here and there, but now it was wine, cured meats, and hard cheeses. People spoke quietly. No one offered food to strangers.

I tried to nap, to catch as much rest as I could, not knowing what the situation would be when I arrived, whether I would be expected to work the dinner shift on the day of my arrival. But sleep was impossible. I was so close now that I felt like everything I saw through the window belonged to my new life—each chalet, each cow, each distant peak. I would see these again, I thought. Soon I would know these places. I would learn them as I was starting to learn each new world I entered. Through food.

Everything about Victoria Jungfrau signaled grandeur. The sprawling rectangular building, long and white, had a massive central tower with a slate-roofed dome.

Wrought-iron balconies covered its facade and overlooked a perfectly trimmed green at the center of town. A man wearing a white jumpsuit clipped away at the hedges in front of the hotel.

In my broken German, I asked for the staff entrance, and the man pointed his clippers toward the back.

The rear of the building had been updated to make it into a modern, highly functioning point of entry, with concrete loading docks and corrugated steel ramps for all the food trolleys that came and went. In the office inside, a young woman in a dark suit rose from her desk and put out her hand.

"Hello, Herrn Samuelsson," she said. "I am Simone. *Wie geht es Ihnen?*" How are you?

She gathered up a handful of the other new guys who'd been waiting in the conference room and led us on a tour of Victoria at breakneck speed, mixing German and English the entire time. She took us to the staff dormitory, a separate building, so that we could drop our bags in our rooms. Mine was small and immaculate, and outfitted with a single bed, a clothes cupboard, and a sink. A single window cast a ray of afternoon light onto a cracked mirror above the dresser, and the walls showed the scuffmarks of interns who'd come before me. I loved it.

We reconvened in the hall and walked back to the main building. More than two hundred guest rooms and suites spread across three stories and, below them, a lobby floor that was nothing short of palatial. I took note of the stained-glass windows, gold-framed mirrors, fountains, atriums, and elaborately carved moldings I wasn't likely to see again. Finally, we passed a dining room far more opulent than Belle Avenue's, with upholstered chairs and coffered ceilings, sparkling chandeliers, and columns carved from marble. Suddenly, I saw Belle Avenue for what it was, a hotel restaurant, wedged in off to the side of a lobby, rather than a grand space intended for its purpose from the start.

"You'll see the kitchen soon enough," Simone said, "but now we go to the staff cafeteria, where you can wait until Chef Stocker is ready for you. It will be twenty-five minutes." Simone left us with a brisk good-bye and good luck. *"Auf Wiedersehen. Viel Glück."*

The staff cafeteria was called the Chatterbox, and its food line reminded me of elementary school, with trays at the start and a shelf to push them along as you picked out your meal. A mix of round and rectangular tables, eight-tops and six-tops, filled the dining area. Picture windows and French doors led to an outdoor terrace with additional seating.

I walked over to the tables, where one guy was sitting by himself, kicking back with a magazine.

"Can I sit here?" I asked in English.

"Of course," he said, with a wide, welcoming smile.

I liked Mannfred right away. He was from a town just on the other side of Lake Thun, where his father had a small restaurant that served traditional Swiss food. While Mannfred was tall and blond and just as polite as every Swiss person I had met, he had a warmth that made him stand out from the rest. He was happy to speak to me in English, thanks to having spent a year as an exchange student in Australia, and we chatted easily. To me, Mannfred was a veteran—he'd been at the hotel a full month already, and he was willing to explain everything I needed to know, from where the bathroom was to which chefs had the worst tempers. We all got the *Zimmer Stunde*, the room hour, he explained, and the one chance each day to fit in all of your life—laundry, letter writing and, if you'd been out the night before, sleep—between shifts. By the end of that first conversation, he'd invited me to go mountain biking with him. I'm going to like it here, I thought, even as I turned him down.

"I don't have a bike," I said.

"We can always get you a bike to borrow," he said. That was Mannfred; he was a problem solver.

After precisely twenty-five minutes, Simone returned to round up the newbies. She led us to the kitchen, which was bigger than any I'd ever seen and gleaming with sleek, pristine equipment. Tony at Belle Avenue had given me a heads-up about the Swiss and their machines before I left. "Just look at their watches," he had said. "They're like that about everything. Perfectly engineered and machined. Nothing's ever more than a couple of years old. You'll see."

I saw. We were there in the lull between lunch and dinner service, so everything had just been wiped down and I couldn't smell anything except for the faintest odor of detergent and bleach. Nothing. How could they possibly have produced hundreds of meals a couple of hours earlier with not one hint of garlic or lemon or butter lingering in the air?

We stood in a cluster filling the central aisle of the kitchen. A door opened, and in walked a man trailed by a half-dozen cooks. Never mind that underneath the skyscraper-high chef's hat, he was shorter and older than the others, slightly stooped and walking with a trace of a limp:

he was in charge. You could tell from his bearing, the way he set the pace and the others fell in behind him, the way he stopped short knowing that they were keyed to his every move. He wore a spotless white apron, its strings crossed and brought around to the front, where they were tied in a bow above his thick midsection. His chef's coat and knife-creased black pants were perfectly clean and pressed, and he wore a pair of black Doc Martens boots. His name was embroidered on the left side of his jacket, Herrn Stocker, and sticking out from the breast pocket was the bowl of a small gold spoon.

Simone spoke. "This is Herrn Stocker, everyone. Chef?"

Herrn Stocker gave Simone a nod—gratitude and dismissal combined in one quick tuck of the chin—and silently looked over the lot of us. Once he got to the end of our line, he gave a second nod of dismissal. Somehow, all of us knew not to move. Instead, we waited as Stocker made a quarter turn and continued down the main aisle of the kitchen and back out the door, his pack of chefs silently falling in behind.

⌖

I slept fitfully in my new quarters, relieved when the alarm clock began ringing at six the next morning and my day could finally begin. The formality of my new home had started to sink in, and as I crossed the back courtyard between the dorm and the cafeteria, I looked down and gave silent thanks to my mother for her obsession with ironing. My chef's coat and pants barely showed the wear of the thirty-hour road trip they'd just been through. On the other hand, the turquoise Converse sneakers, one of two pairs I'd brought along, looked a lot less cool than they had in the Belle Avenue kitchen.

Thirty minutes before my shift began, I walked into the Chatterbox for breakfast. Unlike my first visit, the cafeteria was jammed with people and the tables had self-selected into tribes. Busboys sat with busboys. Cooks sat with cooks, never more than a couple of stations above or below their own. The dining-room waiters, decked out in black suits and ties, sat with their backs straight and their cutlery properly lined up next to their plates. Those who I would later learn were the Portuguese dishwashers and cleaners sat together, their language an easy singsong compared to the harsh, guttural staccato of German that surrounded them.

The only free agents in the room were the so-called international students, in from Mumbai and Tokyo and Buenos Aires. These were either hospitality junior execs sent by their companies to learn from Switzerland's renowned hospitality industry, or rich kids whose parents were indulging a whim or desperately investing in something to keep "Junior" occupied. Members of this group didn't observe the hierarchy; they sat wherever they wanted.

The food in the cafeteria line looked good—not the sloppy-seconds that kitchen staff often got—but I could already feel my stomach tensing, so I grabbed a coffee. I took my cup to a table where a guy wearing a cook's uniform was sitting. He looked to be only a few years older, so he couldn't be too high up on the food chain.

"*Grüezi*," he said, offering up the Swiss-German version of "good day." His greeting was formal, not the *hoi* I had already heard buddies our age calling to each other, but he was welcoming when I asked if I could join him. Jan came from the town of Thun, thirty minutes to the northwest, at the opposite end of the lake of the same name, and he'd been at Victoria for about eight weeks. I asked what the kitchen here was like, and his bottom line was a warning.

"If you work hard and stay out of trouble, he'll leave you alone."

"Who?"

"The boss," he said. "Mr. Stocker."

"Mr. Stocker?"

"Shhh," he whispered. "Not so loud. Don't say his name." Jan looked over at the wall clocks hanging above the newspaper rack. Four identical clocks were mounted beside each other, each displaying a different time. Each had an engraved plaque below it. *Paris. Moscow. New York. Interlaken.* The last clock read six-forty-five.

"We've got to go," he said, stacking his plate, glass, and coffee cup onto his tray.

I followed Jan at a pace most people would consider a jog. When we got to the kitchen, it was already in full action mode—chefs running this way and that. Then I heard the loudest scream I had ever heard in my life.

"Mr. Blom," Jan whispered. "The sous-chef."

Blom was yelling at one of the cooks for messing up an order of eggs; then, with an exasperated look, he threw up his hands and turned. In our direction.

"Look busy," Jan instructed, so I ducked into the nearest walk-in and began to arrange the vegetables. After a few minutes, I peeked out. Even more people were in the kitchen now, and they'd started to gather under a large bulletin board that had a schedule grid at its center. All conversations came to an abrupt halt when the door to the executive chef's office opened. Herrn Stocker entered the room, stopped just under the schedule, and addressed us.

"The new *commis* group, please."

We lined up and one by one stepped forward, said our names, got our assignments, and dropped back into formation. So much for avoiding the army, I thought as the guys before me took their turns.

Blom, the sous-chef, announced our stations as Stocker stood and watched.

The kid before me, Johannes, got posted with the *saucier*, more or less the most desirable station in any kitchen, the one with the most prestige, the one that gets credited with taking any dish from competent to transcendent.

When my turn came, I stepped forward.

"Marcus Samuelsson," I said, somehow getting the words out without choking.

Blom consulted the clipboard in his right hand. *"Kräutergarten,"* he announced.

Herb garden? I might as well have been sent to Siberia. I said nothing and stepped back into the line.

Victoria's garden was a plot about three times the size of a large home garden, and at least a third of it was dedicated to herbs. The rows were neatly divided by wood-chipped paths, and at the end of each row, a metal marker bore the name of what was planted. My chef's whites stood out against the bright morning sun, but also against the green coveralls of the four permanent gardeners I worked alongside. I saw the other gardeners weeding, so I bent down and pulled up weeds, too, until the head gardener, Herrn Banholzer, appeared. Banholzer, a wiry man in his late fifties whose sun-soaked, leathery skin reminded me of Uncle Torsten and other men I knew who lived more outside than inside, gathered us around a row of empty service trolleys.

"Here is what we'll need today," he began, reading from a pocket-size notepad. Each gardener had to fill a trolley or two, and each trolley had a specific destination: for room service; for the main kitchen; for the smaller kitchens of the cocktail lounge and the spa; and for any special offsite events.

In less than a minute, I was in the weeds. It wasn't that Banholzer's accent was hard to understand, but he spoke quickly and with a flatness that made it hard to build a context in cases where I didn't know the word.

"Samuelsson, you will prepare the trolley for the *entremetier*," he said. "*Kartoffeln*. Two boxes . . ."

Not a problem to understand that *kartoffeln* was potatoes, thanks to my grandmother's tendency to sprinkle German words into her speech. Nor was *rhabarber* a problem, since it sounded so much like the Swedish word for rhubarb, *rabarber*. But *erdbeeren*? What the hell was that?

I pulled a scrap of paper out of my back pocket, the stub of a train ticket, and started to take notes. This new word I wrote out phonetically and circled it. By the time Banholzer finished with me and walked off, I had about ten words circled. I could have asked him to translate as he went along, but that went against the universal rule of kitchen work: Stay invisible unless you're going to shine. This was not a shining moment.

Fritz, the youngest of the gardeners, patiently helped me

decipher the mystery words. When we got to *erdbeeren*, he laughed.

"Look down," he said, and there was a patch of strawberries at my feet.

"Erdbeeren," he said.

The garden wasn't where I wanted to be—in fact, I would have died if the guys at Belle Avenue knew I was out picking fruit instead of cooking—but that didn't keep me from enjoying the work. The weather was beautiful and everything smelled good, including the dirt. I snapped off the outer rhubarb stalks from their plants, dug up the potatoes and carrots, and snipped off the freshest, leafiest stems of the herbs: sage, thyme, rosemary, mint. To pick the fava beans, I reached through the gray-green leaves on the plants' bushy stalks to snap off the pods.

After harvesting, I washed off the loot in one of three outdoor sinks and arranged it all carefully on the top tray of my trolley. Following Fritz's lead, I wheeled my full trolley to the door of Banholzer's office, a little room next to the toolshed, with big windows and a door that looked out over the beds. Banholzer had a pair of half glasses that he wore on a chain around his neck. To inspect my trolley, he balanced the glasses on the end of his long nose and went box by box, shelf by shelf.

"One more box of potatoes," he instructed when he'd finished giving my work the once-over. "And then take it inside."

During that afternoon's break, I sat in the Chatterbox with Fritz and had a coffee. I told him I'd messed up by not picking enough potatoes.

"No way Banholzer could have let you go without criticizing something," Fritz said. "But he didn't *reject* anything you'd picked? He didn't throw anything out? That's unheard of." I beamed. I may have been relegated to being a garden gnome, but I was going to be the best garden gnome that they'd ever seen.

I must have been doing well enough, because after one week, Blom announced at our morning huddle that I would switch to Herrn Thoner, the *entremetier*. The *entremetier* station prepared cooked vegetables, soups, eggs, and nonmeat entrées.

I was finally back on the front lines.

One of my good friends in the Victoria kitchen turned out to be an Irishman named Gary Hallinan. Like so many of the Irish men and women I would meet in restaurant kitchens over my career, he was friendly and generous and easy to get along with. Gary—who had jet-black hair, pale skin, and a smile that cut deep dimples into his cheeks—never let the stress get to him. In fact, just exchanging a few words with him had the invaluable effect of bringing my blood pressure down. He was from a hotel family, had earned a degree in hotel management, had already worked at Dublin's posh Shelbourne Hotel, and would eventually go on to a very successful career in San Francisco, but the truth was that he wasn't much of a cook. At Victoria, his time in the kitchen was just a part of learning the ropes, and he approached it sportingly. One day, while trying to sharpen his knife against a long steel, Gary slipped and cut his arm pretty deeply.

The first-aid station was right outside Stocker's office, so Gary walked over and sat down on the floor in front of the office door as he waited for treatment.

Eventually Mr. Stocker came along, and as he came up to this injured man, blood everywhere, Gary looked up at him, and in the middle of what was probably true shock, still managed to keep the hierarchy front and foremost.

"I'm sorry, Mr. Stocker," he said. And then he passed out.

Stocker stepped over Gary, saying nothing, and went into his office, shutting the door behind him.

Which is not to say that Stocker wouldn't get vocal when he saw a screw-up in process. In another kitchen disaster, not long after Gary, a kid named Otto was put in charge of grinding meat for the day's meat loaves. Otto was German, so he had no problem understanding instructions, but he was distracted by the pressure, and in what would turn out to be his last day, he took a shortcut. Otto used a metal ladle to push the meat through the grinder. At first it worked well enough, but on one pass, he pushed the ladle too far down into the neck and the auger blade caught it. Otto didn't let go fast enough, and his arm was stuck in the machine, twisting his hand downward toward the pulverizing auger. The second that Otto realized he couldn't retract his arm, he let out a howl. Out of nowhere, it seemed, Stocker showed up and slammed off the power, two seconds before Otto's hand would have been ground into mincemeat. Stocker and a couple of others untwisted Otto's arm from the machine, and the whole while, Stocker never once asked if Otto was okay; he just berated him.

"Why the hell are you using the wrong tool?" he screamed.

"What were you *thinking?* You were *this close* to losing your arm! Are you trying to get our department in trouble? Trying to get me fired?" I simply turned my back and got to stirring a veal stock, wondering how Stocker could get onto the scene so fast. I came to learn that a great chef keeps an extra eye on the lightweights, the lazy, and the nervous.

They were all dangerous, to themselves and to others, and Stocker couldn't afford to let them screw up. You don't lose your arm in a typical office job. And because of that, his sous-chefs were given the power to fire anyone they found wanting. Often, this was the druggies, the guys who spent all their time off up in Zurich—the best place to get drugs— and who showed up for the morning shift in sunglasses. No hard evidence was required, but the sous-chefs must have had some eyes and ears in the dorms, because in all my time there, when they picked someone to dismiss, they were never wrong. And when people got fired, they were erased. No one reminisced about them openly. No one even said their names.

Another way of weeding out the weak links was through on-the-spot tests. You might be going along in your shift, and suddenly Stocker would stop at your station and instruct you to perform a task.

"Chiffonade of basil," he'd bark, arms crossed. "*Sauce beurre blanc.*"

If you didn't respond fast enough or well enough, you were put on notice. If your game didn't shape up immediately, you were gone.

The key, I realized, was to do the work and keep your mouth shut. This was easy for me on both fronts. I loved the work and I could barely speak the language.

I wasn't a Boy Scout. Like everyone else at Victoria, I went out at night once the dinner shift ended, and definitely had my share of fun. But no matter how late I'd been out, I showed up at work the next morning an hour early.

The kitchen at dawn reminded me of a soccer field before a big match. The grass is perfectly mowed; the field is empty of people but full of anticipation. It was the calm before the day's storm, and I used that time to get a jump on my tasks but also to study the menus and notices posted outside of Stocker's office. The menus were in French, Italian, and German, so I brought along my pocket dictionaries and my journal and I copied each one down, from appetizers to desserts, looking up whatever I didn't understand. I didn't want Stocker to see me, not that there was anything wrong with what I was doing. It was just that the less you put yourself in his line of vision, the better.

Just as I had stayed late working at Belle Avenue, I put in extra hours before and after my shifts, doing advance prep work in the mornings and meticulous cleanup at night. All I had to offer was my labor and my attention, and I was willing to give both. The only time I skipped out was for what had become, since my arrival, a daily ritual: throwing up. I was so nervous, so determined to succeed, so afraid of failing that my nerves got the better of me. Every morning, I came into work and felt the familiar knot tie itself in my stomach. The knot would soon be followed by bile filling the back of my throat, and it was only a matter of time before I'd have to bolt to the bathroom. I'd experienced the problem now and then at my Göteborg jobs when the stress got too high, but now I was completely without that hometown comfort zone.

For the most part, I was able to keep my nerves under wraps, doing my business quietly and then going right back to work. Until they installed a new key card entry system, and on the day the system went into effect, my card for the kitchen's exit door demagnetized at the least opportune time. I panicked, and then I spewed. As the spilled contents of my stomach dripped down the face of the door, three *sauciers* came along, deftly stepping past while nodding at me and saying only, "*Gute Tag haben*, Mr. Samuelsson." Their eyes said what their words didn't: "Take it easy."

As soon as I felt the first wave of queasiness each day, I looked for an opportunity to leave my station. I didn't want to be noticed, which meant I couldn't be away for more than five or six minutes. Health codes dictated that we leave our aprons in the kitchen so that we wouldn't get any bacteria on them in the bathroom. But if I put mine on a peg, it was like a red flag showing I was gone. So I wore it to the bathroom and left it outside the door.

Which bathroom to choose? When you spend enough time with your head in a toilet bowl, you become a connoisseur, and what you want is the cleanest and least used facility, which meant bypassing the toilets adjacent to the kitchen and instead taking an extra ninety seconds to go down a long hallway that led to the bathroom by the administrative offices and loading dock. Running through the halls would get you written up, so you had to walk as fast as possible without breaking the rules.

I took off my chef's coat and hung it on the peg inside the stall, making sure not to touch it again until I had thoroughly washed off. If no one else was in the bathroom, I could proceed undisturbed, but if other stalls were occupied, I would flush as I puked in order to cover the sound. Having food in my stomach made the process go faster, but I threw up even when I hadn't eaten, and the dry heaves took longer and were more physically taxing as my body cramped harder to expel what wasn't there. I carried mints in my pockets just for this daily episode, but I was careful not to pop in so many that I froze out my palate. Balancing my new confidence with my anxiety was not easy.

Wash off, pop a mint, coat back on, apron on, speed-walk back through the hall, and back to the station as if I'd never been away.

CHAPTER 13

Stocker

Every Sunday morning at eleven, the staff on duty convened in the kitchen for a fifteen-minute meeting known as *assemblé*. Stocker's sous-chefs would lay out a platter of good cold cuts and open a bottle of wine. Stocker used the time to announce who was getting promoted, how he felt last week's special events had gone, and what was on the schedule for the week.

When you have a *brigade* of sixty people working for you, you need a consistent method of letting them know what's going on. The wall postings and daily sous-chef meetings got some of that job done, but for interns like me, *assemblé* was a rare chance to hear directly from the general's mouth—and in a setting where he was not yelling at you for some mistake you'd made. This was no holding-hands moment, of course. The hierarchy of the kitchen was zealously maintained, even in meetings: line cooks and *commis* stood in the back of the room and said nothing.

My favorite part of *assemblé* was when Stocker talked about upcoming events. Because he had traveled so widely, he took a real interest in the international travelers who made up more than 80 percent of the hotel's guests, and he would tweak the menu accordingly. On a week when we had several Arab parties coming in, he would tone down the pork entrées and amp up the vegetables and fish. When a group of wealthy Japanese people came in for a week of skiing, lots of sticky rice and exotic mushrooms suddenly appeared on the menu. He was very clear that our guest population was not just one type of person, and we did our job well not only when they were happy with what they had ordered, but when, before they had arrived, we had the experience and ingenuity to figure out what the guests might want, before they knew they wanted it.

When Stocker sensed how many customers were making special requests that had more to do with health than palate, he developed a spa-cuisine submenu and hired a full-time dietician. The presence of Margrit, the dietician, a beautiful young woman with dark hair and blue eyes, completely threw the rest of us. She was not only the rare female in the kitchen, she was a female with privileges: she worked out of Stocker's office, she was the only non-chef to sit in on our meetings and, most surprising of all, Stocker never yelled at Margrit. He listened to her and valued her opinion. She helped Stocker tweak the menu, and together they composed new dishes that would be attractive to guests with diabetes, heart conditions, and various food allergies. Heart-healthy symbols on menus are commonplace now, but in the early nineties, it was practically unheard of even in finer hotels. I was a cocky nineteen-year-old at the time, and back then, I dismissed the guests who asked for special menus as finicky or unadventurous, not real eaters. But Stocker's example nurtured my respect for guests with unique dietary needs, and for chefs as smart businessmen. More important, watching my boss interact with Margrit taught me an invaluable lesson for an up-and-coming chef: he didn't live to torture us—he lived to give the guests the best service possible.

CHAPTER 14

Carina

Three weeks after I'd arrived at Victoria, I was in my room during afternoon break when someone came to tell me I had a call at the communal pay phone at the end of the hall. *"Hej, Marcus. Det här är Sven, Carina's pappa."* Why would he be making such an expensive international call to his daughter's ex-boyfriend? The minute I got on the phone, I sensed trouble. Carina wouldn't get out of her bathrobe, her father explained. She had been depressed ever since I left, and he and Kikoko, Carina's mother, were worried. The only thing that might lift her spirits was if she came down to Interlaken for a visit.

To be honest, I didn't want her to come. But I had been raised to be respectful of my elders, so I couldn't find a way to say no. At nineteen, how do you tell a man that your relationship with his daughter is over and that you are working now and no longer want his nice but needy daughter to be part of your life?

"I'm working fourteen-hour shifts," I said in a feeble attempt to dissuade him, but he was insistent. It'd be a short visit, he promised. We hung up the phone with the agreement that she'd arrive by the end of that week.

When I returned to my room, I paced back and forth trying to sort out my thoughts. (In my room, that meant three steps one way, three steps back.) What had I just said yes to? What kind of message would it send to the management of this elite Swiss resort that I was trying to desperately convince that I was more than an able kitchen laborer? I needed them to see me as a chef in the making, not a black Swedish kid with a girlfriend and one foot back in Gburg. That would not be a good look. Not a good look at all.

Carina came and, unexpectedly, I was happy to see her. Somewhere between home and Interlaken, she'd climbed out of whatever funk she'd been in, and I have to admit: It was a kind of relief to be around someone who knew me well, who could speak Swedish and catch me up on life back home. And, of course, to sleep with each night. But I also didn't want anything or anyone to get in the way of my work commitments, and I told her as much. She had to lie low. "If you go out, use the side exit," I told her. That was the door least likely to put her in the path of one of my bosses. "Or wait here and do your thing. Whatever. Just be cool, okay?"

I'd half hoped Carina would stay in the room, writing letters and reading. But she was too curious, and she headed out almost every day to wander around the town or take day trips: a boat across Lake Brienz one day, a funicular ride up to the view-filled Harder Kulm the next. Half the time, when I came back to the room during my afternoon break, she would be gone, and I wouldn't see her until after my shift, when we'd either hang out in the room or head over to Balmer's, the hangout popular with English speakers, where she charmed everyone we met.

One afternoon on her seventh or eighth day, after I'd put my laundry in the dorm washer, Carina dropped her bombshell.

"By the way," Carina said, "I'm applying for a job here."

I flipped. "You're kidding, right?"

"I talked to this nice girl in human resources, and she said they'd be very interested in hiring someone who speaks Japanese." At least 20 percent of Victoria Jungfrau's guests were Japanese; how perfect to have on hand a pretty girl who spoke French and Japanese, not to mention English and Swedish.

Carina searched my face, waiting for it to mirror the excitement she felt, but I was having a hard time faking enthusiasm. I was on a carefully plotted path to finding success as an international chef. I was on rung two of more than two dozen I'd have to climb before I reached my goal. I couldn't bear the thought of being thrown off course by a girlfriend I no longer wanted in my life. This is not good, I thought. This was not the plan.

"Fine," I said, finally relenting. "But no one here can know we're dating."

Carina was not daunted by my tepid response. "Okay,"

she said. "I'll come back in the fall and put in a formal application."

∽

Most of the letters that came to my wooden mail slot outside the Chatterbox that summer were from Carina or my family. I wrote to them, too, but most of my correspondence was devoted to job inquiries. I sent letters inquiring about kitchen positions all over the world. This was in the pre-computer days, and word of mouth was the way job news traveled. A new *commis* would come in with glowing reports of the last place he'd worked, and ten eyebrows would go up as his peers made notes to themselves to follow up. Anywhere I saw racks of tourist brochures, I picked up pamphlets from hotels and applied for work. I had a rule, though: only three stars or more.

"Why set the bar so high, Marcus?" my father would say. "*Three* stars? Why not take something easier to get into and work your way up? Why make it so hard?"

My logic was simple: I wanted to learn from the best chefs so I could be the best, maybe eventually open my own restaurant. The letter writing, my painfully slow typing on a typewriter, and the proofreading all felt like a nightly round of *mise en place*. Everything had to be just so. And yet, for every twenty I sent out, I'd get one response, usually a curt "not right now." When I saw the stationery from Nice's famous Hotel Negresco, I immediately put it in my back pocket and counted the minutes until afternoon break, when I could open the letter in the privacy of my room.

"Monsieur Samuelsson," it began, and right away I could

tell this letter was not a simple rejection. It was much better than a "not right now." If I were to find myself in Nice, it said, I was welcome to come to their kitchen and see what positions were available. The Negresco was home to Jacques Maximin, the executive chef who had made the hotel's reputation and produced scores of great young chefs: Alfred Portale, one of the leading figures of New American Cuisine, who had cooked alongside Julia Child on TV and was famous for New York's Gotham Bar and Grill; Joachim Splichal, who won the Best California Chef from the James Beard Foundation; and the innovative master pastry chef known as "Mr. Chocolate," Jacques Torres.

As soon as I could score a couple of days off, I hopped on a train and headed south. All along the way, I alternated between reading the French cookbook I'd brought along and calculating my next steps. Once I got the Negresco job, I would not cut short the Victoria contract—that would be a no-no. But as soon as it was up, I'd go to Nice, and from there, maybe I'd head for Paris.

I walked from the Nice train station to the palm-tree-dotted waterfront Promenade des Anglais. The Negresco sat at the center of the Promenade, among a strip of art deco palaces, all of them looking out onto the Côte d'Azur and its brilliant blue waters. In the late-afternoon light, the sun low enough to illuminate the building's magnificent belle époque facade and its unmistakable pink dome, I steadied my breathing and reminded myself to put one foot in front of the other.

Once I was inside, in carefully practiced French, I asked for the kitchen.

"The chef is not here," one cook said. "Come back in an hour."

I wandered along the beachfront, too distracted to appreciate the women sunbathing topless in their rented beach chairs, waiters bringing them cool drinks and fresh towels. When I returned, I got the same answer.

"Chef is not here. Come back in an hour."

The third time I walked into the kitchen, I was steered to an imperious man in his midforties with a half-buttoned chef's coat and a tremendous beak of a nose that he raised up in order to look down at me.

"Who are you?"

"I'm Marcus Samuelsson, here from Victoria Jungfrau." I showed him the letter. "I'd like to work for you."

His expression bordered on amusement.

"*Non*," he said. "We don't have anything." And then he walked away. I felt that he'd read my Swedish name but didn't expect to see a chef with my skin color.

Common practice was to humor the *commis* who'd traveled from so far with a tryout for a day or two—kitchens could always use an extra hand—but I wasn't being extended even that courtesy.

I left, devastated. There were other beautiful hotels along the Promenade des Anglais, but I wasn't willing to take second best. Or maybe it was that having spent all my bravado on the Negresco, I couldn't risk being rejected by a second-tier hotel just because of the color of my skin. *Forget about it*, I thought, and caught the next train back to Interlaken.

I made it a point not to dwell on the matter of race. I believed in my knife skills, and my sense of taste, and my capability to listen and to get things done. I was never afraid of hard work. Every place I'd worked in so far was a success for me because once I had my whites on and started working, there was no doubt that I would be the last man standing, regardless of whom I was up against. One ignorant chef who couldn't see past the color of my skin was not going to stop me. I'd go back to Victoria, learn everything I could, and, eventually, people would have no choice but to say yes.

⌐⚬⌐

With Carina back home and out of the picture, I had been able to return my full focus to work, and my reward was to be moved to a new station every couple of months, exactly the kind of exposure I'd hoped for. *Entremetier, viande, pâtissier*—these were not simply descriptions anymore; they were essential elements of a magical experience that started when a guest checked in.

During my stint with the *entremetier* (cold appetizers), I learned to make a delicious summer avocado soup, creamy with coconut milk, garnished with pink grapefruit and pink peppercorns.

When I was on *viande* (meat), I sautéed a knuckle of veal with carrots, onions, and garlic, deglazed it with white wine, then cooked the juices down into a rich, meaty syrup.

With *pâtissier*, I made hundreds of raspberry and champagne mille-feuille, each one garnished with a scoop of champagne sorbet, each plate adorned with a swirl of buttery caramel glaze. Mormor always asked me what it was like to dine in a five-star hotel restaurant. I told her that I still didn't know. But I did know that to cook at Victoria was to go to bed every night with a taste of perfection on your tongue that lingered, even after you had brushed your teeth.

Mannfred liked to say that if you wanted to make it in Stocker's army, you had to match your heartbeat to his. Stocker was a Picasso in the kitchen: gifted, egotistical, bullish, and brutal, but an artist through and through. On the other hand, Paul Mooney, a cantankerous and exacting Brit, was a heat-seeking missile. It just so happened that he was a chef, but one imagined that the experience of working for him would be the same if he ran a basketball team or a crew of bank robbers: you did what he said, and you did it quickly. If you wanted in with Mooney, you had to buy into more than his vision—you had to fall in, lockstep, with his methods. What Mooney excelled at was breaking staff the way cowboys broke down wild horses. This put him in good standing with Stocker, but with almost no one else. The cheese manager did not appreciate Mooney reducing the young woman in cheese to tears when she wrapped the Stilton and the aged cheddar in the same plastic wrap. She thought she was conserving materials; he thought, and he told her quite publicly, that she appeared to have been born without a brain, and was putting the hotel's very reputation on the line, besides. We chopped, cooked, and tasted our way to perfection because we ran on fear: fear that the chef would not like our work, fear that the chef would not like us, fear that a single misstep could get us humiliated or, worse, fired.

Mooney combed through the kitchen staff and picked out all the outcasts and English speakers for himself. Our crew had Jews, Asians, women (believe it or not, still a rarity in the kitchen), and me, a black Swede. Maybe he figured that if we'd made it that far without the advantage of being in the majority, there was a chance we had both resilience and ambition, both of which he demanded. He would forgive inexperience, but he had no patience for laziness, and there was no room on his team for drunks or druggies. He would dismiss you just as easily for the hint of impropriety as he would for a rotten performance.

Working *garde manger* was part finesse work and part butcher shop. The first time I volunteered to break down a whole lamb, Mooney laughed at me. But none of the other *commis* had volunteered, and I could tell he was impressed, at least enough to let me fail on my own initiative. On the next meat delivery, I went into the meat locker and asked for help, working step-by-step under the watchful eye and loud mouth of Franz, Mooney's *chef de partie*. When Franz revved up the chain saw and handed it to me, the buzz of the motor brought back the turbot incident at Belle Avenue, but wimping out was not an option. When he wasn't calling me an idiot, Franz actually imparted useful information, like why it was important to cut in the refrigerated room so that the fat would stay cold and firm. If it warmed up enough to melt, that was when blades could slip. He showed me how to remove the filet, kidneys, and sweetbreads with a small knife, and how to saw down the bones for stock. Everything had a purpose and a destination.

We got to the leg, which needed to be deboned, filled with thyme and garlic, and set aside for the *saucier*. I plunged my knife into the flesh, rooting around for the bone.

Franz yelled. "What's in that woolly head of yours? I know it's not a brain!"

He took the fillet knife from me and cut *along* the leg muscles rather than through them, lifting out a miraculously clean bone at the end. I loved this part of my time in Switzerland. There was so much knowledge in Stocker's team, from the top on down to the line cooks. A guy like Franz could talk all day about my Afro or my lack of brains, but I didn't care, because I was learning to butcher from one of the best. Once that knowledge was in me, it belonged to me. I could take him or leave him.

⌒⚬⌒

Of all the kitchen's stations, the *garde manger* did the heaviest lifting when it came to banquets. Other stations had their responsibilities, but we prepared the bulk of the food: platter upon platter of sausages and cured meats, sliced cold calves' brain on beds of lettuce and herbs, chilled cream of asparagus soups, smoked halibut with horseradish cream, and eggs in aspic, all of it beautifully laid out on tiered, linen-covered tables. Mooney had a special eye for flourishes, so we also learned how to chain-saw ice blocks into eagles, mold sugar gum paste into flowers, and carve elaborate designs into the rinds of melons.

The first time Mooney handed me a felt-tipped marker and told me to cover a plate in plastic wrap, I thought he'd gone off the deep end.

"Draw your food," he commanded, by which he meant he wanted the vegetables artfully arranged. "If you've arranged your veggies beautifully," he explained, "when it gets to the meat guy, he will respect the plate more. He won't just push everything aside to get his filet on there."

I'd been wrong when I said Mooney was merely a drill sergeant who served Stocker's vision. I would eventually learn that all chefs worth their mettle have their own style and their own passions, but every single one of them can go from zero to jerk quicker than the average Joe.

You have to be willing to be a jerk in the kitchen. Otherwise it's not worth it: the years of apprenticeship, the never Wall Street–level money, the ungrateful diners, the misfit miscreants you count on to execute each service flawlessly, not to mention the prima donna behavior of all those raw ingredients—the coquettish egg whites that may or may not fluff properly for you today; the potatoes that may decide that today is the day that they will burn, not crisp; the tomatoes that didn't ripen because of an unexpected heat wave. As a chef, you are at the mercy of the farmer, the butcher, the fishmonger, the weather, and God.

Mooney would send you back to your room if your shoes weren't polished.

"You're not respecting me!" he'd shout. "What the hell makes you think you're prepared for a five-star establishment such as this? Whatever it is, you're sorely and certainly mistaken!"

If Mooney had kicked our butts once too many times in a given week, we'd go to Mannfred's parents' on our day off. His mother would cook for us and coddle us until we were fortified enough to return. Mannfred was one year younger than I was and nowhere near as experienced in soccer, but we played for the hotel's team and helped it win the local hospitality league tournament. Little by little, I could see my grown-up life come together—a lot of work, a little play. My friendship with Mannfred helped me keep the balance.

⌐—☉

I cleaned up the station after service one night, and when I was done, I reported to Mooney so he could sign me out.

"You're done?" he asked.

This usually made me think twice, but on this night, I'd been extra careful, so I stuck to my guns.

"Yes, Herrn Mooney."

"You're ready? Really? You think you're ready?" he kept asking as he inspected each shelf of the walk-in. When he got to a plastic tub of aspic that I'd carefully wrapped and rewrapped, he stopped.

"Are you sleeping, Samuelsson?" he asked. "Were you out too late last night or something?"

I'd dated the tub, as we did with all perishables, but I got the day's date wrong and had put down the twenty-second instead of the twenty-first. A ten-minute rant ensued, in which Mooney accused me of wanting to poison the guests when we served them bacteria-ridden aspic. He let me know that he thought I was lazy and useless, and maybe that's how we did it in Sweden in our simple country restaurants, but poisoning the guests was not the policy at Victoria Jungfrau. About the fourth time he mentioned the idea of poisoning, he lifted the tub off the shelf, ripped off the plastic wrap, and tipped it over onto my feet.

Mooney continued at full volume, and in another minute or so, Stocker stuck his head through the doorway to see what the commotion was. This did not quell Mooney in the slightest.

"Herrn Stocker," he said, switching from English to German. "Mr. Samuelsson has decided to be lazy today." Stocker glanced at the pink gloppy mess around my feet and then turned to Mooney.

"We need to go over the menu for tomorrow. I'll be in my office."

I spent the next hour recleaning the walk-in, and rewrapping and redating each container, then enduring a second thorough inspection, which ended in a grudging dismissal.

To endure such humiliation didn't get easier after a year of working with him, but I did learn to make fewer mistakes, and every day started off with a level playing field, which is to say that everyone else who worked for Mooney had just as much of a chance as I did of being on the losing end of the daily terror that Stocker unleashed on the team. I also understood that Stocker needed his sous-chefs to be paranoid and to transform their fear into rigid control. Stocker terrified Mooney, Mooney terrified us, and we got the job done as quickly and efficiently as possible so that he didn't have to micromanage each station.

By November, I was slipping up only enough to be chewed out once a week. Since some guys were getting berated hourly, this was a huge improvement. I was finishing a lunch shift one afternoon when I got called into Mr. Stocker's office. Now what? I wondered. As I walked—fast but not so fast that I could be accused of running—I scrolled through my last few shifts the way people say the dying watch their lives flash before their eyes. I knocked.

"Herrn Stocker?" I said.

"Mr. Samuelsson. *Wie geht es Ihnen?*" How are you?

I said nothing in response. How was I supposed to answer? Mr. Stocker had never asked me how I felt about anything before. There was more than a desk between us. He sat there with his gold spoon and his tall pleated hat, his crisp pants and jacket. I had certainly learned how to be cleaner, but I was still a mess, and I couldn't stop thinking about the fish salad I had left out in my rush to get to his office. So much for going a week without Mooney yelling at me.

Stocker cleared his throat and then spoke. "Mr. Samuelsson, *Sie sind ein guter chef.*"

I translated and retranslated what he'd just said. Was I getting it wrong? No. He'd told me that I was a good chef.

"We have watched you be able to work with others, and your effort is good. When you come back from the winter break, Victoria would like to hire you as a *demi chef de partie*. I have suggested you. I am not sure if you are going to make it, but I'm willing to give it a go. Go to human resources and they will handle the details." He picked up a pen and looked down at the papers on his desk.

I did nothing. I said nothing. Twenty seconds must have passed, and he looked up at me.

"That is all. Why are you still here? *Raus! Raus!*" Out! Out!

I walked out in a daze, and all I knew was that I needed to double-check with Mooney. If he told me this was true, that I was getting promoted to *demi chef de partie* of the fish section at twenty years of age, then I would actually believe it.

I got back to the *garde manger*, and when Mannfred looked

at me, he raised his eyebrows. "Uh-oh," he said. "What happened?"

"Not now," I said, looking for Mooney. I found him by the walk-in.

"So what did Chef say?" he asked.

"I think he wants me to be *demi chef de partie*."

"Of course he does. I told him to give it to you. We've put you through it to test you. Do you think this stuff just happens? As far as I'm concerned, you owe me. And I'm gonna hold you to it."

The plan was that I would work through New Year's Eve and then leave Victoria until the spring. I had to exit the country to renew my visa, and while I probably could have filled the time by working at Belle Avenue, being in Switzerland had made clear for me that I only wanted to work abroad and in kitchens with truly international and diverse staffs.

In anticipation of my six-month Victoria contract ending, I'd been sending letters up to my Göteborg connections every week looking for help with where to go next. Stocker himself offered to find me a placement between my Victoria contracts, but I wanted to show that I had juice—at least a drop or two—in my Göteborg world. Finally a Belle Avenue line cook hooked me up with a placement at Nordica, a Swedish-owned hotel in central Austria. I'd bracket Austria on either side with a week of R & R back home, just enough time to spend with my mom and for her to wash my clothes, to let my grandmother stuff me to the gills with her cooking, to hang out with Mats, and to pick up a few shifts at Belle Avenue. After all, I wanted to show off what I'd learned.

CHAPTER 15

A Short Stay in Austria (That Will Change My Life)

A series of night trains took me north and east to Bad Gastein, an Austrian spa town with a long winter tourist season, thanks to its radon-rich springs and ski slopes that held a snow cover long after the other resorts had melted down to dirt. Unlike Interlaken, Bad Gastein didn't attract much of an international crowd—no former higher-ups from the Marcos regime or Gucci-loafered Ferrari owners in sight. Bad Gastein was an Austrian destination for Austrians— the richest Austrians, but the ones happy to vacation within their own borders.

As soon as I walked through the doors of Nordica, the hotel where I was supposed to work, I knew something was wrong. There should have been the clatter of silver and glass in the front of the house as waiters set tables and refilled condiments for lunch. But there were no waiters. No linens on tables, no silverware, not even any salt and pepper shakers. I found the manager, a distracted Swede who told me that the renovation had "fallen off schedule"—something to do with the plumbing. No one could tell when the restaurant would reopen.

My interim gig was gone.

I now had three months to fill before my second Victoria contract started and only enough money in my wallet for a night or two in a hostel. Even more urgently, I had the sense that if I didn't fill my time with cooking, the guys back at Victoria, including Mannfred, would pull ahead of me. Three months was a lot of learning time, and goofing off would only hurt my prospects.

It was like soccer drills: there were a thousand ways to skate by, to fake your way through them without giving 100 percent effort, but you were only cheating yourself. No one was going to chart my course for me; the cooking world didn't work like that. I had to find my own way.

I walked down the hill from the hotel to the center of the village, down the winding streets lined with four- and five-story buildings that stood shoulder to shoulder as if huddling against the bitter winter winds. I can figure this out, I told myself; I just need to think.

I wandered around town until I spotted the Elisabethpark, a gigantic yellow-stucco hotel with four stars on the plaque by its front door. The building had a regal yet worn quality to it: The twenty window frames on each floor held sparkling panes of glass but, if you looked closer, the white paint on their frames was chipped and fading. The domed awning over the front entrance showed fatigue where the metal frame had rubbed too long against the fabric. I saw no obvious staff entrance—it would turn out to be down a hidden alley—so for my first and only time, I passed under that awning and entered through the front door.

A bellhop and two desk clerks looked at me when I walked in. In the few extra beats of their gazes, I sensed that familiar shift from "Who's this young guy?" to "Who's this young black guy?" A small, middle-aged woman in a brown dress and black pumps, with reading glasses on a gold chain around her neck, crossed the lobby to intercept me. She used the formal form of address, *Ihnen*, not the familiar *dir*, to ask if she could be of assistance. At least she respected me enough to throw me out politely.

"I'd like to work in the kitchen," I answered in German, and mentioned what had just happened up the hill. By chance, I was speaking to the owner of the hotel, Frau Franzmaier, who ran Elisabethpark with her husband. She took the Victoria Jungfrau reference letter I pulled out of my bag, held up her glasses without bothering to rest them on her nose, and read.

"I can start right away," I said.

"You speak German and you're not afraid of work," she answered. "Okay, then. We'll give you a try."

⌒·⌒

Memory is funny and, of course, comparative. In a matter of hours, life under Stocker and Mooney began to seem positively cushy. At Elisabethpark, fifteen people did the work of sixty, and I worked six days each week, not five. I started at eight in the morning, worked straight through till four, downed a quick staff meal, and zipped up to my room to rest. By five-thirty, I was back in the kitchen in a fresh uniform—which would be damp and dirty by the time the kitchen closed at midnight.

The payoff for those fifteen-hour shifts was that I jumped several rungs up the ladder. I was given the vegetable station right off the bat, which meant there was no one between me and Mannfred, the executive chef. I was Chef's right hand, and Heidi, a talented chef from Berlin who worked the grill, was his left. By the end of the first week, our trio had established a rhythm: How much we spoke correlated to how fast the orders were coming in, and when Chef asked if we were ready—*"Bereit?"*—I could tell from his inflection whether he was cueing me up to fire a new order or asking me to step in and plate with him.

Frau Franzmaier was our bridge to the front of the house. She burst through the swinging door to the dining room a hundred times a night, plucking a white smock off a hook and putting it over her nice clothes as soon as she came into the kitchen. If it was slow, she'd have a few sips of wine from a straight-sided juice glass and gossip with Chef about this purveyor or that competitor. If it was busy, she would call out orders through the small microphone across the counter from Chef or dip into the back room to retrieve fresh napkins, then shed the smock and head back out to charm the guests.

At Elisabethpark, we did not look to France as the core of our cuisine. We didn't bow down to truffles or put foie gras on a pedestal. Instead, we looked to Austria itself, to goulash and dumplings and noodles and freshwater fish like lake trout and perch. This was a bold revelation.

I learned the regional variations in Austrian cuisine, from Vienna's *beuschel* ragout made from calf lungs and heart to the local *krutspätzle*, a side dish of flour noodles made with sauerkraut, pressed through a strainer, and sautéed with butter. *Salzburger Nockerln* became my favorite dessert: its meringue peaks echoed the surrounding Alps, and the warm vanilla sauce spooned on top was said to be the melting snow. We put flecks of smoky Tyrolean bacon into dumplings and, of course, served loads of *tafelspitz*, the dish that all Austrians love the way Swedes love their herring. *Tafelspitz* was aged sirloin, preferably from a young ox, simmered with parsnips and carrots and spiced with paprika, dry mustard, and cayenne, then served over buttered noodles. I liked it instantly, but I couldn't help wondering how much better it would taste if it had lingonberry sauce to cut through the rich, savory broth.

My shifts might have ended at midnight, but the buzz didn't wear off for another few hours. Some nights I staggered back to my room to record the day's menu in my journal. If I'd learned a new technique for poaching cabbage, I wrote it down. If I'd watched Chef roast a pork belly over potatoes until the drippings practically caramelized them, I wrote it down. If I saw him make button-shaped spaetzle noodles and wondered how they would taste with dill rather than caraway, I wrote down that idea, or made up the recipe and recorded it, step by step, amount by amount.

Of course, I was also a twenty-year-old guy, not a monk. I

found a way to exist outside of this cycle of work and reflection. A couple of times a week I'd hang out with my Austrian comrades at a local pub to relax while we argued over whose job was harder, whose burns were more serious, and who almost went down during service. My story of the Aspic Massacre definitely won me a spot in the Screw-Ups Hall of Fame.

A couple of Austrian girls eventually wandered into our crowd, and I recognized one from the workers' entrance at Elisabethpark. Brigitta worked as a chambermaid. She was a few years older than me and lived above the laundry room. She didn't seem to mind my kitchen German, and, like everyone I met in Austria, she seemed intrigued by this black Swede who'd dropped into their midst. Brigitta was beautiful like an old-fashioned movie star; she reminded me of the women in my mother's photo albums from the 1940s. She was from a tiny village in the part of the valley that grew apples and pears, and she paid attention to me as I struggled to make myself understood.

⌐•⌐

The months in Austria instilled in me a deep appreciation for hard work, and the power of a regional cuisine. In some ways, those Austrian dishes were my first real experience with soul food. Elisabethpark might not have been a five-star restaurant, but I saw that warmth and camaraderie and dedication could produce outstanding food just as well as the cutthroat competition that fueled Stocker's kitchen staff. With fewer resources, we pulled off a different five-course tasting menu each night, as well as a new à la carte menu, handwritten by Frau Franzmaier every day.

In late March, on one of my last days off, I sat in a coffee-house by the town's waterfall, at a table by the front window. Swedes may drink more coffee than any other Westerners, but Austrians know how to serve it. Waiters bring a glass of water and a chocolate to go along with your order, and the coffee is always beautifully presented, served in a glass on a saucer, the foam peaked just so. A *Franziskaner* was a latte made with whipped cream and a double espresso was called a *kleiner schwarzer*. I could never order *schwarzer* espresso or think of the color black without butting up against the memory of *schwarzkopf*, a slur I'd heard from Swedish skin-heads growing up back home.

I had laundry to do and I was overdue to write a letter home, but I was there because Brigitta had left a note under my door that morning, asking me to meet her. I hadn't seen her since the night we hung out at Gatz.

Maybe she wanted to hang out some more, I thought.

I didn't see her come in, so I was startled when she put her hand on my shoulder. She was as pretty and elegant as I remembered: light green eyes and long brown hair with bangs that came down almost to her eyelashes. She had deep dimples when she smiled, but she was not smiling now. She didn't even sit down.

"*Ich bin schwanger*," she said. *I am pregnant.*

If there was any conversation after that, I don't remember it. I was barely twenty years old. I still felt like a kid. How could I be a father? To a baby? To anyone?

After Austria ended and before my second contract with Victoria began, I'd scheduled ten days at home in Sweden, and I now dreaded every one of them. I had gotten a girl pregnant, and as much as I wanted to pretend it hadn't happened, it had.

When she broke the news to me in that café, I was stunned into silence. My brain worked overtime, trying to wriggle out of the reality: Why did this happen to me?

For a second, I considered "doing the right thing"—marrying Brigitta, this woman I hardly knew, and spending the rest of my life in Austria, not a place where many black Swedes from Ethiopia have been known to put down roots. I'd get a job as a line cook somewhere, maybe at Elisabethpark, and that would be it. But before I could even finish articulating that scenario in my head, I was past it.

I couldn't do it.

Brigitta made it clear she didn't need or expect marriage. She had a big family and they would be supportive of her as she raised the child.

"I thought you should know" was pretty much all she said.

"Okay," I said. "Thank you."

By the time I got back to Gburg, I was no clearer than I had been in the moment. And I was pissed off: I'd done everything in my life not to become a statistic. I'd done everything I could to avoid the negative stereotype of an irresponsible black man. Statistics about high numbers of black men who skipped out on their kids had been part of the nightly news for as long as I could remember, but there was no disputing my part in the situation. Or my stupidity.

"You seem so tired, Macke," my mother kept saying. "I think they work you too hard."

"What's on your mind, son?" asked the father who usually welcomed my rare silences.

I tried to calculate the damage my news was going to cause, but I couldn't. Brigitta could not have been more than ten weeks pregnant when she told me. She didn't look the slightest bit heavier. This is what I told myself, to feel better.

Maybe something will happen, I thought. Maybe she'll change her mind.

CHAPTER 16

Secrets

Summer was one long panic attack. Sometimes I felt like I was going to die . . . or at least that the career I'd worked so hard for was about to die and I was standing by its deathbed, watching helplessly. I said nothing about the pregnancy to anyone at Victoria, not even Mannfred. Not even Carina, who started her job at the same time I returned. She and I were given a small apartment in the dormitory—a step up over the monk's cell I had during my first stint. I didn't tell her about Brigitta.

The only way I managed to keep up the lie was that the restaurant kitchen was such a refuge. My job had changed, but everything else, including Mooney's incessant sarcasm, was just as I had left it, and I happily dove back in.

As *demi chef de partie* for the *garde manger*, I now had more responsibility, more independence, and more of a public face. I not only butchered without Franz standing over me, I was now the one who stood over the new batch of *commis* and came down hard on them when they cut through muscle. I showed them how to fillet fish and how to prep oysters by slitting apart the shell without fully disengaging the flesh.

As I learned how to be a leader in the kitchen, I thought a lot about my parents. They were both leaders in their own way. My father was the oldest child in his family. He rowed his younger siblings in a boat, back and forth to school. One of the few men from a small fishing village who went to university, my father was a leader in his community. Whenever he went back to his hometown, he read contracts and advised the fishermen—men he'd gone to school with when he was a boy—on important business and legal affairs.

My mother only completed ninth grade, but she was the leader of our home. My father had the most advanced university degree, a PhD, a doctorate in geology. But my mother had a finely honed woman's intuition. Again and again, I saw how my mother's emotional intelligence helped our family succeed. My mother managed the finances in our family, and through her careful savings and frugality, she was able to put aside the money that allowed me to travel and do my cooking training. As I began to get more responsibility in the kitchen, I tried to rely as much on my intuition as my intelligence.

When we had breakfast buffets, I worked the omelet station, taking orders directly from a long line of guests and cooking their eggs in front of them. This sounds simple, but we were cooking over portable gas burners that gave out uneven heat. Stocker wouldn't hear of us using nonstick pans; he wanted us to use only the beautifully polished copper pans. He believed that an omelet should be cooked through but never, ever have "color," which meant any omelet with a browned edge was to be immediately discarded. On this point, he was adamant. Finally, you had to have enough polish to be able to do all this while chatting up the guests, most of whom couldn't have cared less if their eggs were a little brown.

After Stocker's meeting broke up one morning, Mooney came back to our station and made a bead right for me.

"He wants to see you," Mooney said.

I hesitated, feeling a wave of panic rise up. What had I done?

"Now!" Mooney barked.

Stocker barely looked up from his desk when I walked in. I didn't dare sit down in the chair across from his desk unless I was asked. I was not asked.

"You speak English well, Mr. Samuelsson," Stocker said in German. I wasn't sure if he meant it as a question or a statement, but I decided to answer in English.

"Next to Swedish, it's my best—"

"I have a colleague in Gstaad," he interrupted. "At the Grand Hotel, which is very busy in the summer. He needs cooks. Victoria is Switzerland's leading hotel, as you know, and as such, we must also lead the way in staff. I am sending you for twenty-five days. You will go tomorrow and when you arrive, you will ask for Herrn Muller."

148

I stood, frozen, while it sank in that I was not in trouble. In fact, to be sent away was a reward. "Thank you, Herrn Stocker," I said. I prepared to launch into how much this meant to me, how honored I was, how grateful, and—

Stocker had no interest in compliments. "Do not embarrass me," he said, and picked up his telephone, dismissing me from the room.

Gstaad was only forty-five miles away, still in the Bernese Alps and so similar to Victoria in its no-nonsense professional atmosphere that within two days, I felt like I'd been there forever. The Grand Hotel had half as many rooms as Victoria and its banquets didn't serve more than a hundred people, so the pace was manageable, and I never felt overwhelmed. As an extra hand, I worked in the *garde manger* and also helped out in the meat station. Because the staff was more Swiss and less international in its makeup, people were even more formal in their interactions with me, but I also noticed that I was treated with more deference and respect, as if the Stocker stamp of approval bumped up my status automatically.

When I got back to Victoria three weeks later, my status went right back down to its previous level; in fact, it almost seemed like the sous-chefs and line cooks above me were now determined to keep me from getting a swelled head. They loaded me down with grunt work and, whenever the opportunity arose, reminded me that I was not out "in the country" anymore, but back in the real world. I didn't care. I knew I had held my own in Gstaad, I hadn't embarrassed

Stocker, and I'd successfully added one more notch to my chef's belt.

But the better I got at my job, the less I liked it. Let me rephrase that: I loved working for Mooney and Stocker. Stocker's innovation with technology and technique made all of our lives in the kitchen easier, and his expectation of peak performance was one I admired and aspired to. Mooney, despite his crankiness, was a great teacher, and he rewarded effort and talent with extra attention and time. Even Victoria itself had a personality—of grandeur and tradition, all of which was anchored in a beautiful landscape that I was taking full advantage of, thanks to the hiking, biking, and skiing I did with Mannfred and his friends. But I longed to work in a kitchen where the chef's passions ruled. Stocker and Mooney held to the highest standards in the industry, but they worked from a playbook set in stone. French stone.

Sprinkled throughout the international kitchen staff were the rich kids who were never going to cook as professionals but wanted the Swiss hospitality pedigree. You could tell this group instantly: They strolled along when the rest of us dashed. Their hands were baby soft—no calluses, cuts, or burns. You'd never see them pull something out of a deep fryer with their fingers, as seasoned line cooks did. And they didn't want to help, either—they were completely up front about having come to Victoria with no hands-on experience, and also clear about the fact that their futures as hoteliers or managers wouldn't include any cooking. The rest of us watched in awe as they said hello to Stocker when he passed by. They actually looked him in the eye, which seemed to confuse him, and he usually just grunted in response and kept walking. Still, we also had interns from Tehran and Co-lombo and Seoul who loved to eat, and even more, loved to entertain. They rented small houses around town, and the big benefit for me was that those houses had kitchens. Those of us who lived in the dormitories would get invited over for meals, and we'd have Indian naan bread, Chinese fried rice and glazed spareribs, Japanese *nabemono*. The foods we'd eat at those informal dinners were alive with heat and flavor; they had a vitality that spoke to me instantly and far more persuasively than the thrice-reduced cream sauces that took days of careful tending to render just so. Why was there no room at Victoria for those tastes?

I wrote in my food journal almost every night. I tracked what I was learning, but I also started to ask questions, to play with the what-ifs of dishes that were taking shape in my mind. What if you matched turbot with a miso-based stock? What if you put seared salmon into crisp spring roll wrappers? It was not my place to suggest these things openly, but the ideas kept coming, so I kept scribbling them down.

Meanwhile, Carina and I got along on the surface, but we were mismatched, too. She wanted to see us as having a future; my cooking dreams and my secret threw up a wall that couldn't possibly be broken down.

In late November, the news came. A baby girl, born on the sixteenth, five days after my twenty-first birthday. Both mother and daughter doing fine. I was not fine, though, and every time I looked at Carina, every time she told me she loved me, I felt like a bigger jerk had never existed.

The news of the baby arrived just before Carina and I were scheduled to go on holiday with her parents. They were driving down from Göteborg and would pick us up for a trip to France, then take us back to Göteborg for winter break. I'd picked the destination, Monte Carlo, thinking that I might try for a spot at the famed Hôtel de Paris while I was there, which would be a perfect conclusion to my apprenticeship stage.

The night before her parents arrived, I burst. Carina asked me something simple, like whether she should pack this sweater or that sweater, and I spilled my guts. The one-night-stand, the lying, the pregnancy, the baby. She cried and screamed all night; I apologized, got defensive, and then apologized again.

"Hey," I said at one point. "This is completely messing up my dreams, too."

"Why did you wait until *now* to tell me?" she asked over and over again. *"Why?"*

I had no answer for that.

Her parents, Sven and Kikoko, pulled up to Victoria at eight o'clock the next morning, as planned. We threw our bags into the trunk and for most of the drive south, Carina and I sat mute in the backseat, staring out opposite windows. When we did speak, it was not to each other. Our three days in France passed peacefully, if quietly, and I imagine Carina's parents assumed we were burnt out from work and perhaps a little tired of our dip into domesticity. When we got to Monte Carlo, I felt too anxious and mixed-up to walk into the Hôtel de Paris and ask for a tryout. I'll write a letter, I told myself.

As soon as we got back home to Göteborg, I headed over to Mats's house. Lots of boys in our neighborhood went to Mats's dad, Rune, for advice. We felt close to him because he'd coached us in the local peewee soccer league, but he was also just an all-around solid guy who'd listen, tell you what he really thought, and get you out of a jam if he could.

"This is one I can't help you with," Rune said after I finally spit out my news across his kitchen table. "Go to your parents, Marcus. I can't make this go away."

I went home and confessed to my parents.

"Okay," Mom said.

"Okay," Dad said.

This is going well, I thought. I didn't need Rune's help after all. I'd practiced on my sisters just minutes before breaking the news to my parents. (Anna and Linda had squealed with delight. Not helpful.) Now I was in the living room, doing it for real. My father looked down at the pipe he held in his hand, fingering its smooth stem. My mother had shifted from lounging in the overstuffed chair that sat at the end of the sofa to sitting up straight, letting her knitting rest in her lap. The silence lasted too long.

"I know a guy who works at La Toscana," I said, trying to show that I'd been thinking things through, "who doesn't have to pay child support based on economic hardship or something."

"No, Marcus," my mother said in a hard-edged tone I rarely heard from her. "You are going to pay. You are going to pay every month."

"I don't have any money—"

"That's okay," she interrupted. "We will pay until you do, and then you are going to pay us back and start paying it yourself. And you are not going to miss one month. I guarantee it."

I'm sure I looked confused; up until now, earning money had been last on my list of career considerations.

"You can still go back to Switzerland and cook where you want to cook," Mom said. "But this is your responsibility, and while we will help you now, that little girl is yours to take care of. Always."

CHAPTER 17

A Promotion

When I got back to Switzerland, Mooney bumped me up to *chef de partie*. At twenty-one years of age, I oversaw ten guys at a time, and I attended Stocker's morning meetings, which were always held in German.

Carina broke up with me, and my social life in Interlaken began to revolve around Mannfred and his friends. Fortunately, I couldn't have cared less: getting out of town and skiing with my guy friends was so much fun. One weekend, seven of us decided to take a ski trip to Zermatt and ski the Matterhorn. Mannfred brought along Sascha and Jorgen, two old friends of his from school. The rest of us were from Victoria: Martin, a waiter from southern Germany; and two cooks, Klaus and Giuseppe.

We needed two cars to fit the lot of us. Giuseppe had an old Fiat and Mannfred commandeered his sister's new car. We left early on a Thursday morning, and in the two-hour drive south, we seemed to be driving straight uphill to the little mountain village of Zermatt. The old Fiat strained once we reached the town of Visp, and Giuseppe worked the clutch heavily as he negotiated the hairpin turns. When the roads narrowed to one lane, we pulled over to the very edge of the mountain every time an oncoming car passed by, and I made the conscious choice not to look down. Instead, I daydreamed. I wondered where I'd go next after Victoria, felt bad about how the years with Carina had ended, but was also relieved to be back on track, careerwise. I wondered if my parents were disappointed in me because of the baby, and I thought about how work, with all its pressure, was now the easiest part of my life, the one place where I could drop every other concern and just learn and taste and cook.

Mannfred hit me on the shoulder. "*Nicht mehr schlafen,* Samuelsson." No more sleeping. We were there.

I was a decent skier by Swedish standards. I'd dabbled in it as a kid and watched ski competitions on television religiously—at that time, one of my countrymen, Ingemar Stenmark, was considered one of the best in the world. But now I was standing at the top of the same slopes he'd sped down, and what had looked steep on television looked like a perfect vertical in real life. The other guys, who'd grown up on mountains like this, took off in straight lines while I launched into a cautious slalom. Mannfred stayed back and skied with me, never mocking, never teasing, and we'd regroup with the others when we reached the bottom and do it all again.

At night, we ate sausage and made fondue. As we drank, we also talked shop: we all decided that Mannfred would one day be the chef of Victoria and the rest of us would work for him. (First, though, he and I would get Mooney to hook us up with a *stage* on a cruise ship so we could see the world.) We argued about which sous-chef was the biggest tough guy and speculated on why there seemed to be a sudden influx of East Germans on staff. We skied six hours straight each day, and after a couple of hours of winding down, we hit our beds hard.

Driving back on Sunday, I jumped in the front seat of the Fiat with Giuseppe. Klaus and Sascha climbed in the back. We were in a hurry: we had to get the other car back to Thun in time to catch a train to Victoria, and the Swiss guys said the Sunday train schedule was spotty. Driving downhill was just as tricky as driving up, with the additional challenge of ice slicks that could combine, dangerously, with the down-hill momentum. Jorgen had won the poker game on our last night, so his prize was to drive Mannfred's sister's car. No one else cared who drove, but Jorgen had just gotten his li-cense, so every turn behind a wheel excited him. Giuseppe passed Jorgen whenever he had the chance, then Jorgen would make a comeback on a wide flat stretch and overtake our car. The rest of us shouted and pointed whenever one car passed the other. We stopped to gas up, and while our tanks filled and a light rain began to fall, we stood under the tank shelter. Giuseppe and Jorgen got into a playful competition over whether Italians were the best drivers in the world.

With full tanks, we climbed back into the cars and the game began again. I settled into the front passenger seat, thinking about the stiff muscles I'd be taking into work the next day. Giuseppe and I had a perfectly unobstructed view of the other car as Jorgen sped past us to get in first place. Jorgen was still at an angle to the main road when a large sedan suddenly appeared, coming straight at us. Neither car could stop or slow down in that millisecond of visibility, and the sedan slammed into the new car. Mannfred, unbelted, flew out the side window on impact, and the car spun three times before coming to a stop, wedged up against the side of the mountain. I saw Mannfred land at an awkward angle, his body making the dark equivalent of a chalk outline in the snow. He was hurt. It was bad. But he was alive.

It took thirty terrible minutes for the ambulance to arrive. Each minute was a bomb, in which our lives slowly ticked away, exploded, and then slowly began ticking again. I knelt by Mannfred while we waited and he lay still, taking shallow, awful breaths. We alternately screamed for help and cried. Blood and glass were everywhere.

Martin, who had been in the backseat, stumbled out of the car in shock. He'd have many stitches but came out with no broken bones. Jorgen would never walk again. The driver of the other car died on impact.

Mannfred died in the ambulance.

I got back to Interlaken at two in the morning and somehow fell instantly asleep. When I woke up, it was noon, and as I remember it, there was no sun, only gray and dark. Stocker was in his office, and I sat and talked to him. For the first and only time, we had a long conversation that had almost nothing to do with work. We talked about the accident and about Mannfred.

"It's time for me to leave," I said, at the end, and Stocker did not argue.

"Take a couple days off for the funeral, then come back for a week to finish up," he said. "I am very sorry about this, Marcus."

I had no idea he knew my first name.

PART THREE

MAKING

MY

DREAMS

COME

TRUE

CHAPTER 18

New York

With my twenty-third birthday fast approaching, I sat down and wrote three letters. The first was to an American talk show host I'd watched during my Aquavit internship. He was edgy and funny and, more than anything else, smart.

"Dear Mr. Letterman," I wrote. "Have you ever considered branching out into restaurants?"

I wrote a similar letter to Oprah Winfrey, who was already much more than just a TV personality and would surely see the wisdom of partnering with me.

"Dear Ms. Winfrey," I wrote. "Nothing could be a better accompaniment to the conversations you have on air every day than a restaurant. . . ."

I had written a similar letter to Aquavit's founder, Håkan

Swahn. "If you hire me," I promised, "I will make Aquavit one of the top ten restaurants in the city."

Only Håkan wrote back.

My plane touched down at New York's John F. Kennedy International Airport, and when I stepped into the terminal, the first thing I noticed were all the black people. They were everywhere. Black gate agents, black flight attendants, black baggage handlers, black cashiers, black cabdrivers. Black people, everywhere I turned. The second thing I noticed was that no one was looking at me differently. No, scratch that: no one was looking at me at all.

Right then, I knew I'd come to the right place.

The apprenticeship I finally secured was in a Swedish restaurant. Despite the fact that it was located in New York, this restaurant was more Swedish in its menu than any I had ever worked in. Aquavit, housed in a former Rockefeller mansion on Manhattan's Upper East Side, had opened back when I was still a student at Mosesson. It was the brainchild of a food-loving Swedish businessman named Håkan Swahn who had settled happily in New York some years before but had missed the flavors of his homeland. In collaboration with the famous Swedish chef Tore Wretman, Håkan opened a restaurant that would be the first in the United States to serve more than smorgasbord and meatballs.

I'd landed the job at Aquavit thanks to my old friend Peter, a former *commis* at Belle Avenue. Peter had gone on to do well, and now he was a sous-chef at Aquavit. He got the executive chef, Christer Larsson, to offer me a nine-month apprenticeship, and so here I was at the airport, with nothing more than a telephone number and an address.

I threw my two duffels into the luggage hole of the bus, handed my ticket to the bus driver, squeezed past a woman nodding along with whatever was streaming out of her earphones, and sat by a window.

My first apartment was on the east side of the island, on Fifty-Second Street and Third Avenue. Peter was not only my direct boss at work, he was my roommate, generously letting me bunk with him and his brother Martin in their second-floor walk-up. Technically, the apartment was in midtown, but really, it had none of the business-world cachet of that label. We were more or less on the edge of the world then, in a tenement apartment so small I slept on the massage table set up in their living room.

"You can stay as long as you like," Peter offered, and while I knew he was generous enough to mean it, I also knew I should find my own place as soon as I could.

Peter's apartment was not far from the restaurant, which was half a block west of Fifth Avenue and between Central Park and the Museum of Modern Art, all easy landmarks. But even with clear directions and a city laid out on a strict and logical grid, I got lost on my first day. I was distracted by everything. Especially the street people. In Göteborg, there was only one man who slept in the street. Everybody knew him and knew that he was rich—he *chose* to sleep there. In New York that first day, I saw homeless people on every block, stationed outside ATM lobbies and supermarkets, some holding Styrofoam cups, some passed out in entryways and alleys. I was so turned around and discombobulated on the first day that even though I'd left the house after lunch and the commute was only a twenty-minute walk, I didn't arrive at the restaurant's doors until after my three o'clock shift began. Not a good start.

In many ways, Aquavit was the most comfortable work environment I'd had in years. I now had the skills to do most tasks automatically, which allowed me to pay attention to the overall rhythm of the kitchen, to the way Chef Christer worked through a week's worth of inventory, putting a glazed salmon with potato pancakes on Monday's menu and, by Friday, offering a tandoori-smoked salmon. The kitchen languages were English and a sprinkling of Swedish; the social culture was Swedish and American, a combination of familiar and relaxed; the flavor palate was in my bones.

On the line, I was able to hold my own from day one. I was more precise and probably a better cook than a lot of the guys, but they were fast and I had to get up to speed. We would churn out ninety covers, "covers" being the kitchen term for a meal, for the pre-theater crowd, something I'd never seen before. In Göteborg, Belle Avenue was practically next door to the concert hall and city theater, but no self-respecting Swede would have considered eating until after the shows. At Aquavit, we got the ticketholders in and out in under an hour, then turned around and fed another ninety people right after that. The first few times I was on a pre-theater shift, I thought, There's just no way—this is where I'll fail and be forced to give up. I was drowning, constantly behind, constantly playing catch-up to the guys around me. So what if I was cleaner? It was speed that counted.

When I was at work, I gave everything I had to Aquavit, but when I was off the clock, I was a full-time student of New York. Here, it seemed, was everything I ever wanted. At first, I tried to make my $250 weekly paycheck go further by buying a used bike to get around. It got stolen almost instantly, which led to my first big American purchase: a pair of Rollerblades. I hardly rode the subway after that. The energy of the city was infectious, and I took to rollerblading all over town on everything but the wettest and iciest of days.

Skating was a way to save money and satisfy a lifelong addiction to exercise, but it was also a way to learn the map of the city, its architecture and topography, its neighborhoods, and, most exciting of all, its foods. To get to work, some days I'd skate uptown first and cut back through Central Park, sailing through the aromas wafting from the chestnut-roasting vendors, the hot dog and shawarma carts, the syrupy burnt sugar of the peanut and cashew men. Other days I'd dip down into the thirties so that I could skate through Koreatown, with its smells of kimchi and its Korean barbecue joints in the shadow of the Empire State Building. All those years of playing hockey on bumpy pond ice were finally paying off.

If I worked the early shift, I'd take off after lunch service and skate down the east side of the island, stopping in the Indian groceries to wander through the spice aisles, once in a while treating myself to something unfamiliar, like the pungent, gummy *asafetida*, which went from having a truly objectionable stink when raw to a pleasant garlic-meets-leeks vibe when cooked. One week I'd try yellowtail sushi in the East Village, and the next week I'd save up money to sample the tamarind-dipped crab rolls at Vong.

My favorite of all the ethnic-food enclaves, though, was Chinatown. New York's was the biggest I'd ever seen (at least until I ventured off the island to discover the South Asian neighborhoods of Jackson Heights, Queens), and I had my first dim sum at Golden Unicorn, a two-floor restaurant a couple of streets below Canal that is so vast and well-trafficked that it will probably outlast any other on the island. Chinatown's curbside stalls reminded me of the fishmongers in Göteborg's Feskekörka and along the Bryggan up in Smögen. There weren't just snails on offer here, but five different kinds of snails that had been graded into three sizes. Some of the fish I could recognize, but many vendors didn't know how or didn't bother to translate their signs into English—besides, the bustling shoppers who jockeyed for service suggested that language was not a barrier to commerce. I went into basement supermarkets on Mott Street where I found entire aisles of dried mushrooms, and varieties of ingredients I'd never knew came in more than one version, like sea salt, which I now saw packaged in different grinds—fine, coarse, and flake—and in colors from white to pink to black.

My old boss Paul Mooney kept me company on many of these adventures—in my mind, at least. I'd look at the dish section of the supermarket, noting the graceful curves of teapots, the thousands of chopstick designs, and I'd recall his instructions to draw our food, to study the gemstones in Bern. "Food is not just about flavor," he'd lecture us. "It has countless dimensions, and one is visual. What do you want it to *look* like? What do you want the customer to *see*? Your job is to serve all the senses, not just their taste buds, okay?"

In the aisles of Kalustyan's, a spice market on Lexington

Avenue that continues to be one of New York's best exotic food sources for everything from farro to Kaffir lime leaves, I'd hold different dry curry blends up to my nose, committing their distinct aromatic structures to memory, but also remembering that they wouldn't release their full powers until they met up with heat.

"Toast your spices in the pan first or don't even bother," Mooney would say when he made a curry for Victoria Jungfrau's staff meal.

☞

Another New York came to me through Aquavit: the New York of Central Park. I found it through Carlos, the Guatemalan fry guy who had fingers made of asbestos and would reach into the fryer to pull out pieces of fish and remain unscathed. Carlos turned out to be a serious soccer player. Plenty of guys in Aquavit's kitchen came from soccer-loving cultures. They had a favorite team or strong opinions of who was or wasn't worth much, but not too many actually played with any regularity. Carlos was good.

"I'll show you where you can play," he offered, and the next day we both had off, he took the train into Manhattan from his Red Hook apartment, where he lived in close proximity to twenty or thirty people from his hometown of Guate, or Guatemala City. "We have better teams in Brooklyn, but this is easier for you."

I towered over many of my Central American teammates, which was the exact and pleasant opposite of my lifelong Swedish soccer experience. Even though I knew no Spanish and some of them knew no English, we were all fluent in our sport. We held our own against a crew of well-practiced Brazilians, then trounced a team of American yuppies whose training was no match for those of us born to the sport.

After the game I saw a group of black guys headed toward me. The smallest of the bunch, a light-skinned guy with a shaved head, looked me in the eye.

"*Svenne?*" Are you Swedish?

"Yeah," I said in English. "Are you?"

Teddy told me he was an Ethiopian raised in Sweden and Israel, and the guys with him were equally international, some part Swedish, some Somalian. The tallest one, a guy named Mesfin, was from an Ethiopian family who had moved to Stockholm. Mes was an aspiring photographer in New York, currently working at a coffee bar and schlepping backdrops at a fancy photo studio in the West Village.

Teddy, Mes, and I started hanging out right away. They were more like me in terms of experience and culture than anyone I'd ever met, and they also knew how to navigate the city. Mes had a coworker at the coffee bar, a handsome Somali Swede named Sam. Sam and Mes roomed together in a quirky arrangement they had with a model friend. The model let them stay in her apartment for free when she was doing the seasons in Paris and London, and it was several steps up from anything they could have afforded on their own: a doorman one-bedroom on Twenty-Fifth and Park. At that point, I'd left Peter and Martin's to stay in a series of word-of-mouth apartments with roommates I didn't know and where my stuff, what little of it there was, constantly went missing. When Mes suggested I join him and Sam in their one-bedroom, I packed my bags and went.

We rotated sleeping arrangements; one person got the couch and two shared the bed. At first we were suspicious of the doorman, assuming he knew we were not legitimate tenants, but he didn't seem to care and opened the door for us just as promptly as he did for the little old ladies with their little old dogs. That apartment was my first home in New York, a place where my Swedish-English patois was the common language.

None of us talked about it—we were guys, after all—but we all felt freer in New York than we had at home; we were no longer such oddballs. We all had other black friends and we had other people of color as friends and everybody did his thing. Everything we moved to New York for was happening for us: diversity, music, excitement, creativity.

CHAPTER 19

Like That, He Was Gone

Jan, the new executive chef and my boss, didn't come from a standard fine-dining point of view, and he couldn't care less about France. Instead, he looked to Latin America, the Southwest, and, to a lesser extent, Asia. He didn't make classical stocks; as a go-to herb, he used cilantro instead of thyme. Avocado was a staple. If the best flavor was to be found in a jar, Jan took the jar. If he could have done Southwest style, Mesa Grill with a Swedish flair, he would have, but the problem was that those flavors were often too far away from each other. There were dishes where you could meld them, like a blue corn pancake with gravlax, but the balance he sought was a challenging one to strike.

What I loved about Jan's food was that it was relentlessly flavor-driven. He might never have been to France, but the upside of that was that he wasn't hamstrung by tradition. He relied on his palate, and he was gifted with a brilliant one. He loved the bold chilies of the Southwest, but he also embraced Asian flavors like miso and galangal, and those seemed to be a natural match with Swedish ingredients. Having been to the source countries for those ingredients while on the cruise ships, I often felt like I had a closer understanding than he did of the flavors he played with, but I was not there to challenge Jan; I was there to work for him. I came in early, worked hard, and kept my mouth shut.

Jan seemed to like me from the start. Maybe it was because I was black; before the end of our first conversation, he made sure to let me know that he was married to an African American woman. I smiled politely, but thought, So what? How is that relevant to me? You wouldn't believe how often people say things like this. What really impressed me about his wife was not her color, but that she did the window displays for Bergdorf Goodman. For a broke but style-conscious guy, Bergdorf's was a fantasyland, and I knew every inch of those windows, studying the fabrics and colors and silhouettes as they changed from season to season. One day, I'll go inside, I'd thought.

Or maybe Jan liked me because he saw I was totally comfortable in my role as a supporter, and he needed support big-time; Jan hadn't become a name yet, and that made it hard for him to draw experienced cooks. Aside from Larry and Jan and a few of their highly experienced Mesa Grill friends, Aquavit's line relied on recent culinary school grads, young guys who might someday be good cooks, but who came to the restaurant with no chops whatsoever.

In my first weeks, Jan regularly invited me out after work to party with him and the rest of the Aquavit crew. "C'mon, Marcus," he'd say. "Join us for one round."

I went out a couple of times, while I was still learning people's names, but I cut that off almost right away. I liked the people I worked with, but I wasn't into the expensive champagne or the drugs that often found their way into late-night escapades. I wanted to be taken seriously, and going out to bars and clubs and strip joints and getting trashed seemed like a good way to end up in an unprofessional situation. Plus, the last thing I needed was to make an ass out of myself in front of my employer. It seemed particularly crazy to me when waiters and cooks would go out with Jan and get wasted. That promised way more downside than upside. If I went out at all, it was with my crew of Mes and Sam and Teddy. If I acted the fool with them, so be it. They didn't sign my paycheck.

I'm glad I drew that line, too. It made everything simpler. I liked where Jan was going with his food, and we talked a lot about how he was going to tweak the menu for spring, what dishes to start introducing in March. My classical training came in handy when we were figuring out how to put a new dish into production, and he was always willing to test a recipe that I'd come up with.

"Show me that duck dish you've been talking about," he said one night after service.

"I'll have it for you tomorrow," I said.

The next morning, I plunged a couple of duck breasts in salted water and weighed them down with a plate to keep them submerged, exactly the way my grandmother taught me to cure meat and fish. Six hours later, I took one breast out of the brine and sautéed it in honey and soy. I served a slice to Jan, and he chewed it, closing his eyes and frowning a little as he chewed.

"Nice, but let's try adding another layer," he said, and we sautéed the second breast, this time adding in lemongrass and Kaffir lime leaves. It was fantastic.

"This goes on the menu," Jan said.

Things were going well for all of us. Jan posted every article that mentioned Aquavit on the bulletin board outside the changing room, and the mentions were consistently positive. Valentine's Day fell on a Tuesday that year, but we were full to the gills, and that put everyone in a good mood. Two days later, Jan came into the kitchen carrying a curly piece of fax paper. "Check it out, man," he said as he handed me the page. It was an advance copy of a *New York* magazine article about Jan and the restaurant, praising his leadership after only six months at the helm. His charisma had come across to the journalist, too, who dubbed Jan an "MTV-style" chef. Jan was glowing.

We had a big pre-theater seating that Saturday night, and our middle station cook called in sick at the last minute. This was a problem. Middle station is sometimes called the *friturier* or "fry cook," and he not only does the frying but also helps out the guys on either side of him, who are usually meat and fish. We were short-staffed, so Jan tapped a kid named Allen to take his place. Allen was a culinary student doing an internship with us. He was probably nineteen years old, and on a good day, he would have been the third-level helper over in the *garde manger* station. He probably saw this as his shot, and besides, how could he possibly say no?

"You can't mess up," Jan warned him. "Not tonight."

"I got it, chef," he said, a little too eagerly. "I got it."

Allen did not have it. He was too young and inexperienced to hold it together, he got swamped, and he went down hard during our early service. He hadn't done enough prep, and he was running out of supplies while diners started to worry about whether they'd make it to their seats before the curtain went up. Allen lost track of his orders, and if he stopped cooking to catch up on prep, a dice that would take a practiced cook three minutes took Allen fifteen, and that was twelve minutes we didn't have to spare. The meat and fish cooks stopped asking for Allen's help, and the rest of us tried to help dig him out, but it was no use. For a good half hour, we couldn't get meals out the door in any semblance of order. Guests complained; pissed-off waiters brought dishes back that weren't cooked right. When that seating finally cleared out, and we had a half-hour lull before regular dinner service heated up, Jan exploded.

"What are you trying to do to me?" he yelled at Allen, who stood in front of the walk-in with his shoulders bowed, trying to take up as little space as possible. Jan kicked at the refrigerator door with one of his Doc Martens. The handle of the walk-in broke off and clattered to the floor. That unleashed a torrent of curses, some now in Swedish, capped off by Jan grabbing fistfuls of Allen's shirt and slamming him into the stainless walk-in door.

"Why doesn't Chef just fire him?" one waiter muttered. "It would be a lot less painful for everyone."

The rest of service was no less disastrous, and when we finally finished breaking down the kitchen for the night, I was more than ready to clock out. Our chef and the usual crew were headed out for drinks, but I politely declined. I was going to sleep.

"See you Monday," I said to Jan on my way out.

Sunday was my day off and that Monday, I headed back into work, as usual. Aquavit was across the street from the Peninsula hotel, and on my way in, I said hi to my pal Joey, the hotel doorman.

"Yo, Marcus," he said as I passed by. "I heard there was an accident at Aquavit."

I didn't pay him much attention, went in the front doors, and signed in. Two cooks came out of the service elevator, heading for the exit—the opposite direction from where they should have been going.

"Where are you clowns headed?" I asked.

"Jan died, man. The restaurant's closed."

Died? The words didn't sink in. I kept moving.

I got in the elevator, went down one flight, and walked numbly through the dining room. The seven-story atrium was as beautiful as ever, with water purring down a sculpted copper surface against one wall and a giant mobile suspended above, a colorful smattering of kites borrowed from the Museum of Modern Art. Once I stepped into the subbasement, I saw Adam, the restaurant manager and one of Jan's closest friends, sitting on a stool, alone. Adam never sat still, but there he was, staring blankly, holding a cup of coffee in both hands but not drinking it, tears running down his cheeks. Then I got it. Jan was gone.

CHAPTER 20

Life After Death

"*Vi sitter alla i en knepig plats här,*" Håkan said as the two of us sat in the empty restaurant. We are all in a difficult place here. It was only late afternoon, but grief and winter's dark blanketed the room. Someone had brought us a basket of crispbread and a ramekin filled with caviar spread. Håkan dipped a knife into the putty-colored roe and smeared it across a cracker, then left it on his plate, untouched. I pulled the napkin from the place setting in front of me, folding it and refolding it.

Håkan didn't waste words: No one in-house was in a position to take over. It was enough to have gambled on Jan, a thirty-two-year-old first-timer, so Håkan would be going to Sweden in search of someone to fill the position. Could I deal with a new boss?

"Yes."

In the meantime, Larry was going to hold down the fort. He was older, and a natural manager. As for me: Jan had come to Håkan only a few days before his death to say he wanted me to become his sous-chef. They hadn't gotten around to telling me, but now here it was. I could take the promotion, but only if I was willing to take marching orders from Larry.

"No problem."

We reopened the next day. Larry, who was probably Jan's best friend, tried his hardest to set aside his feelings and work as if nothing had happened. He kept the team together by writing up the shift schedule, ordering the food, and showing everyone that it was okay to keep pushing forward. For the first couple of days after Jan's death, the rest of us were in shock, distracted, going through the motions. The food suffered.

"Get it together!" Larry shouted. "We've got people to feed."

I honestly believe the restaurant wouldn't have survived if Larry hadn't stepped up and taken charge. He was so steady that Håkan worried he was in some kind of unhealthy pattern of denial, and suggested he take a few days off so he wouldn't crash and burn. Larry brushed off Håkan's suggestion, reminding him that when you come from a rough neighborhood like he had, tragedies happened.

"Listen," Larry said. "Most of my friends from growing up are dead or died when we were kids. This is bad, but I've been through it before. I need to keep working."

Larry was a rock, but there was no way to completely smooth over the loss of his talented, charismatic friend.

Without Jan at the helm, the other guys who'd come from Mesa started heading back to Bobby Flay's kitchens—slowly at first, then like rats fleeing a sinking ship. We lost people every week, and we didn't have the pull in the job-hunting market to bring in anyone new. The staff grew leaner and leaner, and we eventually turned every dishwasher and porter we had into a line cook. I spent a lot of time teaching people how to chop onions without hurting themselves.

To any visitor passing through over those next couple of months, it would have looked like Larry was running the show with me as his right hand. But there were three of us heading up the kitchen, the third person being the ghost of Jan. We'd be working on the spring menu or trying to streamline the workflow, and somebody would always bring him into the discussion.

"But Jan would never . . ."

"I don't think that's where Jan was going. . . ."

"Jan didn't really like . . ."

Larry ran the show and talked to the press and the fish guy and the dishwashers; I worked on the menu and filled in wherever he needed me to. We fell into a good groove, but even though I respected him tremendously, I sometimes felt he didn't understand Swedish cuisine. In fact, he'd never been to Sweden, which made it hard to come up with new dishes. Larry would go on years later to have a great career in Las Vegas, but it wouldn't be in a Swedish place. Sweden wasn't in his soul.

Larry's reference point was New York, and after a month or so, it was clear he was headed back to work for his fellow born-and-bred New Yorker Bobby Flay. Larry said he'd stick with us until Håkan found the new guy, but then he would be gone. I could have left, too, but I didn't want to quit on a place that had been so good to me. Plus, what would I go back to? I didn't have a green card yet, so I would have had to head back to Sweden. I was here; why not try to make it work?

Around the end of April, Larry decided he couldn't wait any longer, and officially left to go back to work for Bobby. Håkan still hadn't found Jan's replacement.

"Can you keep it together for another month?" Håkan asked. "Even without Larry?"

"Yes," I said, not knowing how I would live up to that answer. Håkan flew over to Sweden, Larry left, and I kept the kitchen going, counting heavily on two young guys, Nicholas and another Marcus. Somehow, we kept the walls from crashing down around us.

When Håkan got back, he called me into his office.

"Have you found your chef?" I asked.

"I believe I have."

"Who is it?"

"You, Marcus. I want you to be the new executive chef of Aquavit."

I couldn't believe it. It was what I had dreamed of, but I'd never imagined that I would get to run a kitchen at such a young age. But I reminded myself of my own mantra: Step up to the challenge; don't avoid it. Win or lose, take the shot.

⌒

I was twenty-five years old and in charge of one of the biggest high-profile restaurant kitchens in New York. The liberation of being in New York was that the customers who made up our base didn't have extensive knowledge of traditional Swedish food—they just knew what they liked. I saw that as my opportunity to turn the menu around. I could make the herring less salty; I could add a peppery heat to the smoked salmon; and even in the case of the *hovmästarsås*—a sweet dill mustard sauce, served with gravlax, that was almost a religion in Sweden—I made adjustments, aiming for a deeper, nuttier flavor. Adding actual nuts would have been costly and introduced textural challenges, so I used brewed espresso instead. I started testing out the sauce in dining-room specials, and the response was strong. Eventually, it became the sauce we used for both herring and gravlax. Later, I even took away the chopped dill that had always been a given on the plate. I felt it was a cliché.

As for the dining room, Nils—the new sous-chef I hired—and I poured all our creative energy into developing new dishes. I started by looking through my old food journals, remembering flavors and pairings and preparations from everywhere I'd ever worked, everywhere I'd ever been: I wanted to find ways to incorporate the efficiencies of Switzerland, the soulfulness of Austria, the reverence for ingredients I learned in France, but I wanted to do it with a Swedish accent. The key was to keep seafood at the front and center of the menu. I kept some of Jan's dishes, like his lobster wrapped in pear slices, and began adding my own as soon as I could develop, test, and refine them. We fell into a routine of sitting down after lunch, talking through new ideas and then splitting up to go and work on them individually. Every idea was run through a gauntlet—not only did we talk about how it would taste, but we broke it down into distinct components: How would it look? What was the ideal temperature to serve it at? What kind of mouthfeel did we want it to have?

We both looked beyond food for our inspiration, which was key. I might build a recipe on the idea of being on a boat off the shores of Smögen; Nils would read a book about architecture and start out a concept based on shape. Each of us would take the lead on certain dishes; others were pure collaboration. Nils came up with an amazing counterpoint to our salty, spicy fish dishes: a goat cheese parfait. I rolled salmon in parchment paper and served that with an orange-fennel broth. I made a salmon tartare using a barely smoked salmon, then served it with crispbread and a mustard we'd created. I knew right away I wanted to do a tomato soup with crab at its center. So I slow roasted tomatoes in salt, sugar, black pepper, and garlic, then filled each tomato with crab salad and placed that in the center of a low, flat bowl that held a ladleful of a gingery tomato soup that had the citrus notes of lemongrass. I just knew these flavors would work together, and they did.

Nils and I used every spare moment to keep pushing into new territory, always with flavor in mind. For example, once I'd toppled the *hovmästarsås* god, the door was open for me to try more. From my rollerblading adventures, I knew which Pakistani and Indian stores near Twenty-Seventh and Lexington would have mustard oil or purple and black mustard seeds. If I wanted to make a jackfruit sorbet, I'd take the D train down to Grand Street, do a lightning shop, then zip back up to the restaurant, carrying everything in my backpack. I'd try whatever caught my eye; because these weren't fancy French ingredients, I never ran into cost problems. Bitter melon looked like a cross between okra and cucumber, but it was most definitely neither; lychee fruit, when peeled, looked like translucent eggs; sliced lotus root reminded me of the doilies Mormor put on the back of chairs to protect the upholstery. Some things I recognized from a market in Singapore or a stand in Hong Kong, but when it came to more mysterious items, I'd buy anything once, as soon as I'd established from the seller that it wasn't going to kill me.

Every time I went down to Chinatown, especially in the early morning, the beauty and insanity of the neighborhood seduced me. In summer, the streets were already packed and smelly, even though the sidewalks were freshly hosed down.

When Nils and I found a way to use a new ingredient, the next step was figuring out how to package it. I knew that a word like *galangal* on the menu would make Håkan go bananas, so we had to find a way to hide it. We'd make salmon brushed in miso and wrapped in Thai basil, then serve it with fennel and a broth that used Kaffir lime leaves, lemongrass, galangal, and the Japanese citrus fruit called *yuzu*, and on the menu, we'd call it crispy salmon with orange broth and grilled fennel. Wasabi was horseradish; ponzu was citrus vinaigrette. The key was presenting these things in accessible, understandable terms, which kept customers in their comfort zone. I had a responsibility to the restaurant not to confuse the diner, but I had an even greater responsibility to upgrade the food. It was a delicate balance.

At the same time I was trying to reimagine the menu, I was developing as a chef, and I had more than my share of failures. You could make a mistake back then without it sinking you. Reviewers always came more than once before they wrote their reviews, and food bloggers—who take the pulse of a restaurant every thirty seconds and sound the death knell if they don't like the feel of a napkin—didn't yet exist. One of my more notable disasters was a beef tenderloin dish. Aquavit never was and never will be a steakhouse, so I thought I'd replace the boring, straight-ahead, grilled New York strip we offered with something more sophisticated and gentle. I poached the beef in milk and served it with potatoes and sorrel, a vegetable that seemed just right for late spring and early summer. It is a really great dish—if you have an all-star team in the kitchen. We didn't. To begin with, poaching is a far more delicate process than grilling. It's easy to miss the mark and end up with dried-out meat. With grilling, the texture and flavor that come from charring over high heat cover up a multitude of sins. I was aiming for something more feminine, but the process requires close attention and periodic checking—in other words, a little too sophisticated for a busy Saturday night and the twenty-one-year-olds we had on the line.

After a week of failing miserably, Nils and I agreed to go back to the grilled New York strip.

Throughout the summer, we kept banging and pushing. I had so much food in me that I launched six- and seven-course tasting menus, changing them almost every day. It was an ambitious if not slightly crazy idea for an understaffed restaurant, and we kept at it for the better part of a year, until we started to settle into a rotation of dishes we felt worked, and also when I could see that it was unfair to expect the waitstaff to fully understand and represent the food when dishes flew in and out the door so fast. Håkan knew that we couldn't and shouldn't sustain so many changes, but he also knew the restaurant needed positive energy. I don't regret pushing so hard, because in the back of my mind, I knew this was my moment. Out of the tragedy of Jan's death had come an amazing opportunity to communicate the diverse flavors I was so passionate about.

If Nils and I went too far, it was because we were there to kick ass, and anybody who didn't fall in line either left of his own accord or got pushed out. Håkan put everything he had into supporting our efforts to turn things around, too—he renovated the restaurant's interior, brought in a restaurant consultant, and hired the leading food PR company in the city, the same people who were representing established chefs like Alfred Portale and Rocco DiSpirito. Between the consultants and the flacks and the press, I felt like I was undergoing interrogation: What's your philosophy? What's your food mantra? What's your vision? Where do you get your inspiration?

"I'm just working," I wanted to say, but of course that wasn't enough. I had achieved my dream of becoming the *koksmastare*, the head of the kitchen, and I had to accept the corporate stuff that came with it. Through their efforts, I started to develop ways of talking about my food—that I liked it highly seasoned, that my anchors were Sweden, France, and the world, and that I wanted to create something *different*.

Word started to get out. Editors from *Food & Wine* came in to eat, and so did the great Chicago-based chef Charlie

Trotter, who instantly took a liking to our new direction and became an ally and a friend. Our consultants drew on their deep connections to the American dining scene: they arranged for us to host the meetings of the city's most prominent wine society, to partner in a charity event for the James Beard House, to participate in a wonderful anti-hunger project called Taste of the Nation. Håkan dealt with most of the schmoozing, but he'd bring me out to this person or that group to shake hands and say a few words. Gradually, a buzz was building.

No restaurant ever succeeds solely on the talents of its chef. There has to be a good business model, someone keeping careful track of food costs and management. This was where Håkan excelled. Håkan and the consultant, Richard Lavin, who was serving as the restaurant's general manager, taught me how to be accountable to those points. At our Thursday morning meeting, the three of us would sit in Håkan's elegantly appointed office and talk about long- and short-term goals. I walked into the first meeting without a pen and paper, but never made that mistake again. If linen costs were up, we discussed why. If I wanted new plates in the dining room, where was I going to cut back in order to free up that money? If we talked about a challenge we faced, it wasn't enough for me to say I'd take care of it. *How* was I going to take care of it?

We all pressed on, and then, boom, one day in late September we found out we were going to be reviewed by Ruth Reichl, the top critic for the *New York Times*. The night before, a few of us gathered in Håkan's apartment to watch a local news channel that gave a preview of the review. The minute they announced that Reichl was giving us three stars, Håkan and the rest of my coworkers jumped out of their chairs and shouted. I would have been thrilled with two stars: three was beyond anyone's expectations. There were toasts, there was backslapping, there was some fist pumping. I was happy because they were happy, but the import of the review didn't sink in.

The day after the review came out happened to be one of our wine society dinners. The head of the society stood up to make his opening remarks, and after attending to the society's announcements, he brought up the review.

"When I met Marcus," he said, "I knew he would be the one. I knew when I picked this place for our dinners there was magic in the air."

I thought, This is great; let's all just get back to work. But as soon as the review came out, it *was* magic. I had dreamed of success for so long. I'd left restaurant after restaurant, from Belle Avenue to Victoria and several more in between, because I knew I could do better.

But the truth is that I had no idea what success would look like, feel like, taste like.

When you're the new twenty-five-year-old chef at a relatively low-profile Swedish restaurant and you get a three-star review from the *New York Times*, it's like making a small indie movie and winning an Oscar. The whole world shifted on its axis. In two days, our reservations doubled. The congratulations cards and calls and flowers were endless. Everything opened up in ways little and small. I used to have to argue with my fish guy over our order, which always came to us last on his list of deliveries; now we got our fish at nine o'clock sharp, and it was always the best. I didn't have to argue with any of my vendors anymore; in fact, they began to send new products for me to try, gratis. I was flooded with invitations to all sorts of cooking events and for the best tables at restaurants. We started to get calls from Sweden from cooks who wanted to come over to work. Wow, I thought. This is the way it is supposed to be.

CHAPTER 21

Losing My Father

On August 11, 1996, my father, Lennart Samuelsson, passed away. He was at home in Göteborg; I was at work in New York. He'd been struggling with the aftermath of a stroke, but then he took a sudden turn and was gone. I wanted *desperately* to go home and be with my family. But if I attended my father's funeral, my immigration status would be in jeopardy.

My mother said she understood, my sisters said they understood, but honestly, it would take me years to say that *I* understood the choice I made. All I know is that I did what, by now, came naturally: I crammed my grief and fear into a little box and closed it up until I was ready to deal with it. There was no time, I told myself, to make a meal out of this misery. Nothing could get in the way of my cooking.

That night, I pulled out a copy of the letter my father had written to the adoption agency before he knew me:

April 3, 1972

Dear Maj-Britt!

The Adoption Center in Stockholm, which helps us with the adoption of Fantaye and Kassahun, has asked us to write you and tell you about our family and our living situation. We do it here and with the help of some photographs. First, however, we want to thank you for the work that you perform and wish you success!

We are three people in the family. Father, Lennart, born on Smögen in Bohuslän in 1932, first studied to be a public school teacher. Then studied further for a master's degree. He has had employment as an elementary school teacher, teacher, lecturer, and is since 1969 a state geologist and director of the Geological Survey of Sweden, Göteborg Branch. During three months in 1971, I was a UNESCO expert at the Center for Applied Geology in Jeddah.

My work consists of the production of geological maps, and my work for the next ten years will be in western Sweden. I also conduct lectures and classes in geology at the University of Göteborg. My income is between 5,000–6,000 kr a month [$1,041–1,250 US].

Mom, Ann Marie, was born in Hälsingborg in 1928. After practical school, she was employed as clerk and cashier until 1964. At that time, we bought a house and she has since been a housewife.

In December 1966, we had a foster child, Anna, who was then fifteen months and now is eight and a half years. Her father is colored and mother Swedish. Both live in Sweden but live apart. We have good, although somewhat sporadic, relations with both. We wanted to adopt Anna, but the biological mother has hesitated and we have allowed things be. The biological parents, however, both expressed their desire that Anna should grow up with us. Anna is a healthy and happy child and looks forward with great expectations to some smaller siblings! She has always found it easy to have good friends and playmates.

As a family, we have also a good dog (collie) and an equally nice cat, both very friendly toward children.

We live in a child-friendly residential area, Puketorp, of about three hundred families. There is a surrounding forest, where we hike in the summer and ski and saucer in the winter. A couple of small lakes with crystal-clear waters are also in the woods, where we go skating and swimming. Puketorp is in Partille municipality, one mile east of Göteborg.

Our site is about seven hundred square meters and a mostly flat lawn with a playhouse and sandbox, so children tend to gather with us and tumble about properly, jumping and playing with balls and croquet.

The house consists of three rooms, hall, kitchen, bathroom + basement with two rooms, hall, combination toilet-shower room, laundry room, boiler room. We plan to build a new house next year, on forest land ten minutes down the road from us.

Anna's paternal grandmother has houses on Smögen, so we usually go to the archipelago and the sea when we wish to change from the forest.

Her maternal grandmother and grandfather live in the same residential area that we do, just five minutes away, and they are very good with small children and are retired, so they have plenty of time and also help us if we need babysitting or care of animals when we cannot take them with us.

I do not know if this data is sufficient. If not, please let me hear from you and we will respond again.

Our dearest greetings

Our dearest greetings. My father's letter marked the beginning of our life together—my father and I—and it did not seem right, nor possible, that the journey was over before I had become chef of my own restaurant, before I had proven to him that I could do it. My father and I were meant to taste the world together. I wanted to take him to Jackson Heights in Queens so he could see why they called the neighborhood Curry Heights. I wanted him to try real fried chicken in Harlem. I wanted to chow down on po'boys with him in New Orleans. I imagined us eating hot dogs and drinking beer at Yankee Stadium and conch fritters in Florida. My father was sixty-four when he died. Maybe that was why I took the news with what must have seemed like cold resolve: the numbers simply did not add up. I thought, I hoped, that we had as much time ahead of us as we did behind us. It seemed unfathomable to me that we did not.

When my grandmother died, it had been easier to feel connected to her at work. Any kitchen could invoke the spirit of Helga; the smell of chicken roasting, the smell of fresh herbs, the sound of onions sizzling in the pan could conjure up my grandmother and make her seem close. My father, though, had been an academic, a bit of a taskmaster, a conservative Swedish man who had nonetheless crossed continents to find a son and love him. My relationship with my father was more complicated and the sweetest parts of it—fishing at the summer house in Smögen—felt outside my reach. My father's death left me rudderless; I'd guided myself by him for as long as I could remember. He was the one who taught me how to read a map, bait a hook, make a fire, fix a bike, pitch a tent. He taught me, by example, that some principles, no matter how clichéd they sound, really do mean something. Hard work *is* its own reward. Integrity *is* priceless. Art *does* feed the soul.

I went to work at Aquavit the morning after he died and told nobody about what had happened. I had responsibilities to the restaurant, to Håkan, to my staff and my customers. This is the way restaurants work. No matter what happens in the course of a day—death, birth, celebration, love, ruin—you show up for your next shift. For some people, this becomes a burden, but that constancy over the years has kept me grounded. And it was Lennart, my beloved father, who taught me how.

I talked to my mother every couple of days, worried she would fall apart without Lennart in her life. But she did not; she turned out to be a lot stronger than I'd given her credit for. She kept on, so I kept on. For six months after my father died, I didn't stop working. If anything, to avoid dealing, I picked up the pace. I was working fourteen, fifteen hours a day. I was numb. By then, I'd changed apartments. I still lived in Hell's Kitchen, but Martin had moved in with his boyfriend and I'd moved in with Mes. One night I came home from work. It was late, but Mes was still up. We sat on our couch, watching MTV. We were talking about nothing in particular and, suddenly, I just lost it. I cried, for the first time since my father's death and for the first time since I was a child. Mes sat with me, listening as I tried to repeat every single wise word, funny story, and lesson in manhood that my father had shared with me. When I finally went to bed, it was almost dawn. I knew my father would be with me forever. The life he gave me, the lessons he taught me, would always burn brightly in my head and in my heart.

CHAPTER 22

Creating My Signature Dish

No matter who you are, whether you've got a small-town restaurant or you're an Iron Chef, you want to create a signature dish—one you create or execute in a way that becomes forever associated with you. All chefs put our own twist on the food we serve, but a signature dish requires more than merely customizing. I considered many of the changes I'd implemented at Aquavit to be mere tweaks, whether it was changing the size of the meatballs, pulling back on the smoking of the salmon, or updating a mustard sauce by adding the nutty accent of espresso. In truth, most chefs will never come up with a signature dish, because it takes luck and time and the ability to look at things in a fresh, new way.

One approach to a signature dish is taking something

famous, like coq au vin, and making it so well that everyone knows it's yours. The other approach is to go out on a limb and create something entirely new. That's the exciting route, especially for young chefs. For me, the path to my first signature dish was through foie gras. Foie gras is a specially prepared duck or goose liver. It's got a rich, buttery taste that can be used in dozens of different ways.

I didn't grow up with foie gras; I grew up with my grandmother's liver pâté, which was rustic and grainy, but good. The first foie gras I saw was at Belle Avenue in my hometown of Göteborg, but even that came out of a can. It wasn't until Switzerland and France that I began working with real foie, and in both places, the ultimate expression of that core ingredient was in terrines that took hours to prepare. When I came to America, chefs approached foie differently. They took American-produced foie gras from upstate New York— the idea of it being not only domestic but also local floored me—put it in a pan and seared it quickly, serving it on brioche toast with fig jam, say, or a slice of mango. I loved this taste; it seemed cleaner and it really explained the difference between French cooking (traditional) and American (flamboyant).

The only problem was that everyone was doing it, and I didn't want to be like everyone else.

So I decided to focus on texture and temperature. My first idea was to make warm foie gras blini. These little pancakes—made simply with flour, eggs, and water—tasted good, but the overall effect was too chewy and dry, robbing the foie gras of the velvety texture that was one of its greatest assets. What would happen, I wondered, if I took that blini batter and steamed it in the oven like a pudding? That gave me back the velvet, but the texture struck me as too uniform. I tried one version after another after another. Along the way, in one of our post-lunch conversations, Nils and I debated what the end goal should be, and we hit upon the model of an extremely popular dessert at the time, the molten chocolate cake. These were incredibly rich little cakes that had a crusty exterior and a runny liquid center. You didn't need much of one to satisfy you; in fact, too much would leave you stupefied.

With the molten cake model in mind, I turned to individual ramekins, lightened my batter by cutting back on the egg, and switched from steaming to high-heat baking in order to set the crust. This delivered the contrasting textures I wanted. I felt I was getting closer, but I didn't like having the taste of white flour in the mix, so I replaced that with almond flour. I also found the standard four-ounce ramekins a little too big, so I hunted and hunted until I found a source for cups half that size. In France, I saw the customer often left us holding his sides, almost like, "I'm never going to eat again." I wanted customers to leave Aquavit saying, "I hope I can do that again tomorrow." You have to be careful with this when you're presenting yourself as a luxurious restaurant. It's a fine line between leaving the customer feeling good and appearing stingy.

As I developed my foie gras dish, I played with the seasonings. I adjusted amounts of butter—although it's fair to say there is always plenty of butter involved—shallots, white pepper, cloves, and cardamom. Foie gras works well with a good wine, so I reduced some port, steeped tarragon in it, and then added that reduction to the batter. Then I added a little garam masala, one of my favorite spice blends at the time, to give it a hint of heat.

Finally, I made a test batch. Nils was there to try a first bite when I pulled the tray of ramekins out of the oven, and when we put those first spoonfuls in our mouths, we looked at each other and didn't have to say anything. We just smiled. I had it at last: foie gras ganache.

Over the years, I've served different versions of this dish, infusing it with sea urchin or corn, serving it straight from the hot oven alongside tuna or cool cubes of salted watermelon. I've cooked it all over the world with everything from orange marmalade to truffle ice cream. What stays constant is the texture, the temperature, and the quality of the ingredients. Once I got it right, meaning that it hit all the marks I cared about, I knew I had my first signature dish. I've served my ganache to kings and starlets and three-star chefs and people who simply love food. Everywhere I go, the dish is a hit.

My success in creating signature dishes wasn't just about what I was doing; it was that what I was doing found an audience of people who were curious about the flavors I was chasing. They were willing to chase them, too. As chefs, we definitely are in the memory business: we are creating a memory with ingredients. I wanted my customers to leave my restaurant satisfied but also curious about what made their experience so great. I wanted them to turn to each other during the ride home and ask, "What *was* that?"

Another signature dish started with a trip to Boston. I was driving along the Massachusetts coast on the old scenic highway, and every five minutes I passed a seafood shack promising the best lobster roll in the state. I'd never had one, so I pulled over and had lunch. For months afterward, the memory of it stayed with me. I'd loved the straight-forwardness of it: take some fresh lobster and mayo; put it on a soft, buttered roll; and, boom, that's it. In Sweden, lobster is called "black gold," but at Belle Avenue, we either drowned it in Newburg sauce, a creamy sauce made with milk, paprika, curry powder, and cayenne, or covered it in a thick Thermidor sauce.

I wanted to celebrate the richness of the lobster, not obliterate it. Even the American seaside version struck me as a bit heavy-handed when it came to the mayonnaise used to bind it. I wanted a creamy texture, but not all that oil. At the same time, I didn't want to just plop a pile of naked lobster onto a plate and let it fend for itself. How could I introduce the experience of discovery? I wanted to create the sense of before and after. With the lobster, I had to figure out what that screen could be. Since I was always looking for ways, at Aquavit, to filter food through Sweden, I turned to the idea of pickling, a flavor counterpoint to the richness and sweet-ness of the seafood.

As I had with the ganache, I went through a trial-and-error process until I hit it: lobster rolled in a skin of thinly sliced pickled Japanese plums, a homemade mayo on the side, and a topping of diced bacon and glistening red caviar. This, along with the ganache, became a fixture on the Aquavit menu. I think if they were ever taken off, there'd be a riot, at least among the regulars. And even today, when I make these dishes, I remember the joy of the discovery process.

CHAPTER 23

Back to Africa

Ruth Reichl, then editor of *Gourmet* magazine, called me at work one afternoon.

"Marcus," she said, "I don't think you're going to be able to resist this idea."

The year was 1999 and a young journalist named Lolis Eric Elie had pitched a story idea to *Gourmet:* He wanted to do a feature on me, but he didn't want to rehash the same old stories about my Swedish upbringing and my arrival at Aquavit. He wanted to go with me to Ethiopia, to look at its food through my eyes, eyes that hadn't seen that country for thirty years.

Ruth was right. I couldn't resist this. I'd be gone for two weeks, the longest I'd been away from the restaurant since becoming the executive chef.

"Of course you'll go," Håkan said when I told him I was debating over whether to be away for so long. "You have to."

My immigration status was resolved and my career was on the rise. It seemed like the perfect moment to return to the country of my birth.

We landed at Bole International Airport in the capital, Addis Ababa, the city where my mother died, and I spent the next two weeks falling in love a hundred times a day. Ethiopia has faced terrible struggles and still does, but its ancient landscape and the warmth of the people were unbowed. My birth nation is sometimes called the land of "thirteen months of sunshine," and it was true: one crystalline day followed another. Our decommissioned Russian taxicabs rattled down the city's main boulevards and battled not just other drivers but also herds of goats and sheep and cows, the livestock completely unthreatened by our smoke-belching vehicles. The smell of freshly roasting coffee beans poured out from each little shop, even ones with paintings of computers or hairstyles in their windows. Reddish dust kicked up everywhere and coated everything. The colorfully trimmed cotton scarves and shawls that covered every man's and woman's shoulders were often used as masks, held in place by a hand.

In those two weeks, I saw my own face reflected a thousand times over, which gave me not only a sense of belonging unlike I'd had anywhere else in my life, but also a deep reminder of how fate had steered my life on such a different course. I'd see an eleven-year-old version of me with a cardboard tray of tissues and gum set up at an intersection. I'd see my own face dashing into coffee shops, my own hands using a branch to sweep the sidewalk in front of a butcher shop. I'd see an old and bent version of me, wearing a blanket-like *gabi* shawl in the cool of the early morning, his hand cupped and extended as he chanted his plea for money. *"Birr, birr, birr."*

One of my favorite discoveries was the Merkato, the largest open-air market on the African continent, so big that an entire lane is dedicated to butter merchants, an entire city block set aside for sellers of traditional clothing, woven white cotton with embellished hems. Donkeys were everywhere, standing in for pickup trucks, for dollies, for forklifts. I spent hours in the spice aisles, fingering nuggets of frankincense, buying packets of black cumin or deep orange *mitmita*, just so I could smell them later in the filtered air of my hotel room. Our guide translated and showed great patience as I pointed at one bin after another after another, hungry to know the names of everything. I saw one chili powder blend everywhere and quickly came to recognize the Amharic characters that represented it.

"Berbere," explained the guide, whose name was Fiseha. *Bayr-ber-ay.* "We use it in everything."

In my room that night, I poured out some *berbere* onto a coffee saucer. The blend was finely ground, so I could only rely on nose and tongue, not sight, to parse out the herbs and spices that had gone into it. I wrote a list of the spices in my journal, and the next day I checked with Fiseha to see how I'd done. I'd guessed nine of the dozen ingredients. The base ingredients were obvious: chili pepper, black pepper, and salt. After that, I came up with a list I knew well from Swedish cooking—cardamom, ginger, nutmeg, cloves, cumin, and coriander. Fiseha helped me with the last handful. I don't know how I missed the allspice and the fenugreek, and what

I could have sworn was thyme turned out to be *ajowan* seed, also known as bishop's-weed, which layered in another fiery kick on top of the peppers.

"Sometimes there's garlic," Fiseha told me. "Also cinnamon."

⌒⋅⤙

From time to time, the journalist Lolis would ask if I recognized any smells or sights or sensations. If my sister Linda had been with us, she might have answered differently, but as much as I would have liked to say yes, I recognized nothing. That first trip to Ethiopia was less a reunion than a whirlwind romance. I felt welcomed wherever I went, even when people realized I couldn't speak Amharic. I certainly dressed and acted like a *ferengi*, their word for "foreigner," but they often called out "Habesha" to me, claiming me as their own. I spent one afternoon in a teff terra, a small, poorly lit hut where a five-woman cooperative produced round after round of *injera*, the same kind of spongy bread my birth mother once made. Ethiopians eat *injera* at every meal, using it as both plate and utensil. I watched as they pulverized the teff with a stone, then sifted it into powder. They mixed this with a sourdough starter and water, then set it aside for a couple of days. At the center of the hut was a broad metal griddle that looked a bit like a barstool, a wide drum for a top and set on long legs, but underneath was a small coal fire, which choked the air of the hut, a signal that breakfast was being prepared.

As a chef, it's impossible to be in a new place where serious cooking is going down and not want to try your hand at it. One morning, I watched a woman pour fermented *injera* batter onto the grill in a perfect, smooth spiral, starting at the outer edge of the hot surface, and I smiled and nodded at her until she handed over the dented can she used for a ladle. It looked so simple when she did it, but that's how deceptive expertise can be. My attempts were lumpy and misshapen, and her words of encouragement were delivered with the patient tone you take with a not-so-gifted child. Nothing wrong with being humbled now and then.

The first time I made *doro wat*, my teacher was a seventy-five-year-old woman named Abrihet. Mutual friends had set up my tutoring session, and we met at Habesha, the restaurant Abrihet cooked for that was right off Bole, Addis Ababa's main drag. In the Habesha kitchen, we started from the very beginning by killing a chicken, plucking it, and then gutting it just as I'd perfected in France. We cut it into a dozen pieces, not the eight or ten I was accustomed to, and submerged those in lemon, water, and salt, a brine that may have evolved as much for food-safety reasons as for flavoring. As the meat marinated, Abrihet plunked down a sack of red onions in front of me. I felt like I'd gone right back to my *commis* days. While Abrihet washed the collards that would be an accompaniment, I chopped all the onions myself, pounds and pounds and pounds of them, finely, finely chopped. All I had was a bad knife and a horrible cutting board; I realized how spoiled I'd become, and even though I felt clumsy trying to navigate the divots and dull edge, I figured if Abrihet could do it with these tools, I could, too.

Abrihet looked slightly embarrassed and said something to our interpreter in Amharic.

"What?" I asked him. "What is she saying?" The interpreter looked a little reluctant. "Tell me," I prodded.

"She's embarrassed," he said. "She says it's not the Ethiopian way to have a man in the kitchen. But she says you are not from here; you are a *ferengi*, so it's okay."

We chopped up a little garlic and ginger and divided that, along with the onion and some butter, into two pots.

"She says this must cook for forty-five minutes," the interpreter explained. "With very little heat."

Our next step was to dry off the chicken parts and add them into the onion mixture in two batches. First the dark meat, which takes longer to cook, and then, twenty minutes later, the light meat. Thirty minutes after that, the stew liquid had turned a rich brown. Abrihet put on two more pots of water, one for the greens and one for boiling some eggs. When the greens were ready and the eggs were done and peeled, we ladled the stew onto the center of a big platter that had been blanketed with a round of *injera*. The collards and eggs were evenly divided around the perimeter.

We sat down to eat, and after the ritual washing of hands, we ripped off pieces of *injera* with our right hands and used them to scoop up mouthfuls of stew. Abrihet made a little packet of food and reached over to me, putting it into my mouth.

"This is *gursha*," the interpreter said. "This is a sign of hospitality. She will do this two more times, and then, if you like, you should do the same to her." I could barely swallow before my next *gursha* came, and when it was my turn to reciprocate, I probably dropped half of the food out of the *injera* on my way to Abrihet's mouth. But she didn't mind, and I was too happy to mind. After all, I'd just learned a piece of my past. Like so many of the Ethiopian dishes I learned to make over the years, *doro wat* served a dual purpose of expanding my repertoire as a chef while, dish by dish, adding texture and layers to the African heritage I so longed to know.

⌐⋅⋅⌐

We stayed at the Sheraton Addis, the most luxurious hotel in the country. It was not like Sheratons in the United States; this was a palace, so opulent it was almost uncomfortable, especially since the moment you left the hotel's heavily patrolled gates, you stepped into an open-sewered shantytown, patched-together sheets of tin and cardboard that housed huge, extended families, families who lived with no water and no electricity and nothing but tamped-down dirt for a floor. I had never considered myself more than middle-class, but in Ethiopia, I was beyond advantaged.

I was treated like a prodigal son everywhere I went, pampered and attended to and interviewed by local newspapers and magazines. I could see that our visit meant a lot to the Ethiopians we met, and so, to say thank-you, I felt like I should put on a dinner for our hosts, forty of Addis's movers and shakers and politicos. The hotel staff loved the idea. We set it for New Year's Eve—mine, not theirs, since they operate by a calendar that holds its New Year celebration in September—and the Sheraton gave me carte blanche to use its staff and resources. This was eye-opening. The support team of the kitchen was all Ethiopian, but the chefs were Europeans. This made me stop in my tracks. Here I was in the only country in all of Africa that had never been colonized, a predominantly black country, mind you—and white Germans were in charge of the kitchen crew? I knew enough about the hotel industry to know that this imported upper tier was not the first string. In the international hotel business, the A team goes to America, Asia, and Europe. The B team ends up in the Middle East. The C team gets Africa. I might have gotten more angry, but how could I, when everyone from Klaus, the executive chef, to Tesfahun, the man who ran errands for the lowest level of *commis*, welcomed me so warmly into their kitchen?

I spent most of the second week putting together my menu and inventorying the hotel pantry. Because most of the hotel guests were foreigners, virtually all of the hotel kitchen's ingredients were imported. When I suggested using some Ethiopian ingredients in our dinner, I got blank, slightly embarrassed looks. The Sheraton Addis Ababa, I was told, did not serve Ethiopian specialties. So I borrowed porters from the hotel and we did several Merkato runs to stock up for the big night, which had somehow gone from forty people to sixty.

"Or quite possibly seventy," the concierge said to me with a broad smile.

My second agenda for the dinner, beyond saying thank you to the gracious people at the Sheraton, was to inspire the Ethiopian staff by showing them what one could do with traditional Ethiopian ingredients. I began to think of the meal as my homecoming dinner and decided I would also try to bring together pieces of all the cuisines I knew and loved.

My appetizer was smoked salmon crusted with *berbere*. I wasn't set up to replicate my uncle Torsten's smokehouse, so instead, I quick-cured the salmon, then put it in a makeshift smoking box along with green coffee beans, a little bit of water, and cinnamon. After fifteen minutes I took out the salmon and was satisfied, even proud of the smell—bright and clear like the ocean. I took *berbere* and rubbed it on top of the salmon and served it with *ayib*, the local cottage cheese, chopped dill, and wedges of dried *injera* that could be used as crackers. Out of all the dishes we served that night, this was the biggest hit. Not only because it was delicious but also because people saw for the first time what was possible with Ethiopian ingredients. The rest of the meal carried this theme. I rubbed duck with *berbere* and served it with figs and foie gras and a honey wine called *tej*. For dessert, we did a hot chocolate cake with warm beets and finished it with coffee-flavored honey syrup. Throughout the menu, I honored Ethiopian ingredients, and we did it at a level no one had ever seen before. The Sheraton Addis had a lot of things to recommend it, but Habesha soul wasn't one of them until this meal.

When I got home, spilling over with stories about what a fantastic time I'd had, friends asked me if it had been hard to leave.

"Not at all," I said. "Because I know I'm going back."

CHAPTER 24

My Fourteen-Year-Old Self

There are some facts I am proud of. I was the youngest chef to be awarded three stars from the *New York Times*. I was the second chef to win *Top Chef Masters*. I've been fortunate enough to win awards for my cooking and my cookbooks, and I've opened restaurants all over the world. My proudest accomplishment is the opening of Red Rooster, in Harlem, the New York City neighborhood I now happily call home. And the thing is that none of it came to me in a straight line. Very little of it came easily. This book is titled *Make It Messy* because I am far from perfect. I've made my share of mistakes along the way. Mistakes are okay. What matters is that you take the time to learn the lessons and that you make the effort, when you can, to make them right. As the saying goes, "Never a failure, always a lesson."

Sometimes when I'm at the restaurant or taping a TV show, I think about what would happen if my fourteen-year-old self were to show up at that very moment. What would he think of me and the life that I've made? I know the first thing he would say is, "Dude, what happened to your soccer career?" I would have to explain then how I was cut from the team, that I just wasn't big enough to continue competing in Sweden, through high school and university and into the pros.

But once my younger self got over the disappointment of my not being a professional athlete, I know that he would be amazed that I made cooking—this thing I did on Saturday afternoons with my grandmother—into a bona fide career. The boy I was would be shocked that I was on TV. "Dude," he would say, "how'd you get yourself on TV?" He would be shocked to see me on highway billboards and in ads on the sides of buses.

I know my teenage self would smile with pride to see my grandmother's name and her recipes painted on the wall of my restaurant. The boy I was would puff up his chest and give himself a high five when he learned that I had cooked not only for the president of the United States, but for the king and queen of Sweden, too. Speaking of queens, I know that the younger me would be taken aback by the beautiful woman who is my wife. "She's *gorgeous*," he would say. "How'd you get *her* to marry *you*?"

It all seems so surprising now, but if I look back, I could see that I always had three things that held me in good stead: I was humble, I was willing to work hard, and I loved food.

I'm thrilled that you are reading my book, and I know you're not asking me for advice. But if you're young, here's what I want to tell you. Everyone will tell you to work hard. Everyone will tell you to be humble enough to start at the bottom and be willing to learn from every job you have as you make your way up to the top. Honestly, all that is true and valuable. It's not a cliché. I'd like to add to that advice and urge you to never rein in your ambition. No matter how big your dreams may seem, dream bigger. And don't be discouraged if your dreams start to take a different form. I didn't become a world-famous athlete, but I've achieved the kinds of things my fourteen-year-old self could have never imagined. You will, too.

Acknowledgments

To my two mothers, Ahnu, who sacrificed, and Anne Marie, who always supported my food journeys.

To my father, Lennart, who made me the man that I am.

To my Ethiopian family, who are the anchor to my beginnings.

To Helga J. and Edwin J., who fed me a steady diet of love, tradition, and roast chicken.

To the leading ladies of my life, Anna, Vanessa, and Linda.

To all my soccer coaches, who taught me a strong work ethic and teamwork. It's with failure that we can get back up and become even better than before.

My uptown family, you know who you are. Thank you for teaching me about grace, hospitality, and the importance of history and excitement for the future.

To those who read *Yes, Chef* and told me you took something from it. It makes the journey all the worthwhile.

To the team that makes it happen every day—I couldn't do it without each and every one of you.

And to those who have struggled or are struggling: stay in the game and stay focused. It takes character to be great.

MARCUS SAMUELSSON is an internationally acclaimed chef who caught the attention of the culinary world at the age of twenty-five, when he became the youngest person ever to receive a three-star review from the *New York Times* for his work at the New York City restaurant Aquavit. His iconic restaurant Red Rooster Harlem celebrates the roots of American cuisine in one of New York City's liveliest and most culturally rich neighborhoods. He is also the chef behind Norda Bar & Grill in Gothenburg, Sweden; American Table Café and Bar in New York City; and the Kitchen and Table concept restaurants, all partnered with Clarion Hotels in Scandinavia.

Marcus has written several cookbooks, as well as the *New York Times* bestseller and James Beard Award–winning memoir *Yes, Chef*. He was a winner of Bravo's *Top Chef Masters* and the Food Network's *Chopped All-Stars*. He was honored to be a guest chef at the White House, where he planned and executed the Obama administration's first state dinner, for the first family, the prime minister of India, and four hundred guests.

Marcus lives with his wife, Maya, in Harlem. He plays

soccer on weekends and is constantly searching for the best street food around. Follow him on Instagram, on Facebook, and on Twitter at @marcuscooks.

VERONICA CHAMBERS is a prolific author, best known for her critically acclaimed memoir, *Mama's Girl*, which has been course adopted by hundreds of high schools and colleges around the country. She has written more than a dozen books for young readers, including *Plus* and the Amigas series. She is a graduate of Bard College at Simons Rock. You can visit her online at veronicachambers.com.

Pine River Library
395 Bayfield Center Dr.
P.O. Box 227
Bayfield, CO 81122
(970) 884-2222
www.prlibrary.org